Ghosts of
YORKTOWN
VIRGINIA

A HAUNTED TOUR GUIDE

JEFFREY SANTOS

Schiffer
Publishing Ltd

4880 Lower Valley Road • Atglen, PA 19310

Copyright © 2018 by Jeffrey Santos

Library of Congress Control Number: 2017954759

Designed by RoS
Cover design by Justin Watkinson
Type set in Birch Std/Chaparral Pro

ISBN: 978-0-7643-5513-4
Printed in the United States of America

Published by Schiffer Publishing, Ltd.
4880 Lower Valley Road
Atglen, PA 19310
Phone: (610) 593-1777; Fax: (610) 593-2002
E-mail: Info@schifferbooks.com
Web: www.schifferbooks.com

For our complete selection of fine books on this and related subjects, please visit our website at www.schifferbooks.com. You may also write for a free catalog.

Schiffer Publishing's titles are available at special discounts for bulk purchases for sales promotions or premiums. Special editions, including personalized covers, corporate imprints, and excerpts, can be created in large quantities for special needs. For more information, contact the publisher.

We are always looking for people to write books on new and related subjects. If you have an idea for a book, please contact us at proposals@schifferbooks.com.

Contents

Introduction

Ghosts do exist. They are around us all the time, both day and night. Through the twilight hours, when the world is still, their presence seems more apparent. We may not notice them during the day, when the sun is high and all is bright, but even then we walk in their midst. Those who doubt the reality of this spiritual realm have perhaps never walked the streets of colonial Yorktown after sunset. It is along these historic streets that spirits from long ago linger. They move about the old homes and structures. Glowing apparitions and bloody soldiers peer down from windows above, watching us as we go about our everyday lives. Shadows move about the churchyard and dance among the crumbling headstones. Phantom soldiers yell in the night as they march into battle, accompanied by the eternal echo of cannon fire from the past.

Though the tragic, trying, and victorious echoes of Yorktown's history may not be apparent during the day, they still lie beneath the peaceful, elegant beauty of this colonial town.

Yorktown is a quiet village that sits nestled along the marl bluffs on the south bank of the York River. Once a bustling port town, it is now host to thousands of vacationers each year who come to soak up the sun along the sandy shoreline that was once consumed by wharves and warehouses. The glistening waters the beachgoers swim in and upon which sailboats gracefully glide were once full of British and allied warships, volleying cannonballs at one another in an attempt to send the enemy's ships into the depths of the brackish water. Some of these ships still lie beneath the deep waters of the York, resting on the river bed. Yet the violent history of what lies beneath these waters yields to the beauty of a summer day along this scenic river, as fishermen cast their lines and the laughter of children playing along the shore fills the air.

Along Main Street, the carefully reconstructed colonial structures provide a walk back in time. The scars of these war-torn buildings lie meticulously covered by delicate layers of plaster and brick. Yet a glimpse of some of the more prominent homes, such as the Thomas Nelson house, will reveal evidence of the bombardment of Yorktown's siege in the form of cannonballs that were left behind from America's struggle for independence. Guided tours offered by the National Park Service provide detailed insight for the history buff. Visitors are offered a stroll along the same streets that have been graced by some of our nation's greatest heroes. Learning of the character and valor of those who occupied this town and walked these streets during two of American history's greatest wars can be quite inspiring.

There are also several restaurants at which to stop and grab a bite to eat, along with hotels that offer accommodations for the overnight visitor. Many of these establishments offer a ghost story, as well as some interesting history and good food.

Join me now on a tour through the colonial village of Yorktown. Along the way, we will visit some historic sites and learn about some prominent figures from American history. We will talk about events that shaped the nation, the men who fought for freedom, and those who opposed it. We will venture off into the night to explore the dark side of Yorktown. We will walk along the streets and past the graveyards. If you do not believe in ghosts, you will after you mingle with these ghosts. So grab your camera and voice recorder, because the spirits await us along the streets of colonial Yorktown.

The overpass at Crawford Road at night, c. 2015. Courtesy of Jeff Santos

Crawford Road

Where do urban legends begin? This question is sometimes difficult to answer when it comes to certain locations. Such is the case with Crawford Road. When a location is surrounded by so much history and tragedy, it is possible that many of the specters and phantoms seen in the night can be manifestations from past incidents. Though the common ghost story associated with Crawford Road does not particularly lead one to any historical event, it does make one wonder where its origin lies. Along this dark, winding road there have been sightings not associated with the bridge. People have witnessed Revolutionary War soldiers walking along Crawford Road, along with the sounds of drums and cadence calls. These spirits could be attributed to all of the events and encampments that were once along Battlefield Tour Road, which crosses over Crawford. Let us take a closer look at this road and some of the legends that seem to emerge from its little bridge.

Traveling down Yorktown Road from Newport News, just past Endview plantation, lies a long, narrow road known as Crafford Road. Crafford Road connects Newport News to Yorktown, where it intersects with Goosley Road. At this intersection, the spelling of the road changes to Crawford. During the day, Crawford Road is a quiet little drive through the peaceful woods that border Newport News Park, but deep beneath that peaceful appearance lurk the spirits, both human and non-human, that linger in the darkness. This road has seen its share of tragedy, with murders that have occurred along its dense woodline. However, the focal point of the reported activity seems to be a little bridge that crosses Crawford Road known as Battlefield Tour Road. It is said that a lonely bride who was jilted at the altar fled to this bridge in tears and hanged herself. Many thrill seekers and ghost hunters come to this bridge at night in hopes of catching a glimpse of the hanging bride's apparition. The legend states that if you park your car under the bridge at night and turn off your engine, you will hear the sound of something hitting the top of your car. This is believed to be the feet of the dangling woman, replaying her final moments when she met her demise. Also, there have been several reports of a dark figure with red eyes that appears in front of your vehicle, rendering it inoperable as long as he is present. The dark figure then fades into the night and the vehicle allegedly starts up again. As you are driving away, be sure to glance in your rearview mirror and you may see the glowing outline of the grief-stricken bride hanging from the bridge.

8

Late one night, there were eight local thrill seekers who went to explore this urban legend. As they approached the bridge in their vehicles most were eager to see something paranormal, but one of the girls, Carol, was more eager to leave. Nonetheless, she decided to brave the darkness and the eerie appearance of the graffiti-covered overpass. The group parked their vehicles just short of the overpass and decided to get out of their cars. As the group explored the site, they noticed that Carol had disappeared. They wandered through the woods, calling out her name for the next thirty minutes, but could find no trace of her. Finally, Carol came running out of the woods, very shaken from her experience. The group listened as she recounted the last thirty minutes of the night.

Carol stated that when she got out of the car, Alison asked her to accompany her into the woods so she could relieve herself. Carol did not know Alison very well, since it was Carol's first time meeting her. As the two walked through the woods they exchanged small talk. The conversations suddenly grew eerie, though, when Alison mentioned that she was looking for her mother. When the two girls emerged from the woods into a field, Alison ran to meet an older woman who was standing at the far edge of the field. Alison took the older woman by the hand and the two walked into the field and disappeared.

Startled by their disappearance, Carol turned and ran as fast as she could back to the rest of the group. She told them what had occurred, but the others in the group insisted there was no one named Alison accompanying them that night. No one quite knows who Alison was or why her spirit still lingers along Crawford Road, but it was an experience that Carol will never forget.

The story of the suicidal bride is difficult to trace. Many times legends such as these are passed down from generation to generation by locals. Whether or not it holds any truth is hard to say, but it causes us to wonder why so many people have experienced unexplainable events on this road if it is not true. One thing we can say for sure is that there are historical facts presenting many events that could have left spiritual imprints on this road and the surrounding area. Along Battlefield Tour Road, there are several little historical markers that relay the history of this land during colonial times. The Tour Road presents a peaceful drive that connects army encampments, an artillery park, Nelson's Quarter, and even a French mass burial ground. In areas that hold so much history, it is very common to find reports of spiritual activity. This would explain the sightings of soldiers walking about the area, but what about the dark mass with the glowing red eyes?

Many have reported seeing this dark entity along Crawford Road. The most common sighting seems to occur when someone is parked under the bridge with their car off. It is possible that this entity sees the subject as slightly less able to evacuate under these conditions and decides to approach. Its intentions are unknown. Those who have seen it report feeling extreme fear and anxiety. The dark entity does not emit favorable energy by any means. This figure has not only been seen under the bridge, but it seems to wander about other locations along Crawford Road. A little way up from the bridge, heading toward Newport News, you will find Tower Road intersecting with Crawford Road. This dirt road leads to an abandoned radio station where there have also been sightings of the dark figure with the red eyes similar to the one sighted under the bridge. Those who dare to venture back to the station at night (which is illegal, so do not do it) have seen him standing in the doorway of the abandoned building, peering back at them with his red eyes. What causes this entity to linger along Crawford Road? Could it be that this entity has manifested from the murders that occurred along the road, or from the turmoil and bloodshed of the war?

Many have seen this figure, but few may know where it emerged from. This is a question that I set out to answer along with a few other members of Virginia Paranormal Investigations (VAPI). After five years of taking late night drives down Crawford Road, hoping to catch a glimpse of the hanging bride or the dark figure, we decided to visit the road with a medium to see what kind of insight she could provide. It was around 2:00 am one December night. We had just finished investigating some locations in Historic Yorktown and figured we would take a drive down Crawford Road. We turned on to Crawford from Goosley, on the Yorktown side, and headed toward the bridge. At the beginning of Crawford Road there are a few houses that cast a slight glow from their porch lights, but once one goes beyond the glow of the lights, Crawford Road is pure darkness. The trees and the woods seemed to move along with our vehicle when in the distance our headlights dimly lit up the overpass. As we looked at the bridge an eerie feeling came over us; we knew we were a good ways in the woods at the center of all the reported activity, and it would be quite a disturbing, uneasy walk if the dark figure disabled our engine. We disregarded the chills, as they were probably caused more by our prior knowledge of the legend than any entity that may be present. We looked to the medium, and she reported nothing too unsettling about the bridge. If there was a presence there on previous occasions, it was not showing itself this particular night. We decided to drive down toward Tower Road, close to the site where a murder took place in the late nineties. As we approached the intersection of Tower Road, something caught the medium's attention, along with the attention of one of our other members, who saw something dark moving from the corner of his eye. The medium stated that a tall, dark figure passed in front of the vehicles. She was clearly concerned about the sight she just beheld. She went into detail about the figure, explaining how it was not something that ever walked the face of the earth in human form. She described this dark figure as a guardian that was keeping other spirits trapped there. We, lacking any psychic abilities, were unable to read this far into the figure that had just crossed our path, but we all shared the uneasy feeling about what had just happened, especially given the medium's reaction.

For the next few months I continued research on Crawford Road, and I came across a few individuals who had some experiences to share with me. As I conducted the interviews, I heard the usual reports of the hanging woman and the dark figure, but nothing new. Then one of the individuals referred to the dark figure as a "guardian." This caught my attention, given the experience I had a few months prior. She explained that the guardian watches over the area and is not fond of late-night visitors. She described him as a tall, dark figure that mostly appears near the intersection of Tower Road, exactly where the medium had seen him during our venture just a few months prior. I have to say, receiving these two similar reports, from two completely unrelated people, definitely sent a chill down my spine.

Another report of activity at the Crawford Road Bridge comes from three airmen who decided to embark on a late-night trek to investigate the urban legend. It was a particularly dark night as the three young men turned on to Crawford Road. As they continued toward the overpass from the Newport News side, they shared their thoughts on the vacant road and the chilling feelings rushing through them. When they reached the bridge, they stopped their vehicle just shy of it. They turned off their headlights and squinted into the darkness, examining the graffiti-covered bridge for activity. Shortly into their observation they noticed a light on top of the bridge. At first consideration, they assumed there were some local teenagers up there, probably investigating the urban legend. However, there were no visible cars at the bridge. How did they get there? As they watched what they thought was a flashlight, it moved along the top of the bridge and slowly began its descent down the path leading from the bridge to the road where their vehicle was stopped. They still could not see who was holding the light, if anyone. As they observed, the light kept its course, moving toward them. At this point they thought it may be a park ranger or police officer coming to instruct them to leave. The light came right up to the rear window, where one of the airmen was sitting. He lowered his window and the light shut off. No one was holding it, and all was quiet along Crawford Road. After the immobilizing shock had faded they scanned the woods and road with their flashlights but did not find a trace of any reasonable explanation.

We still continue to travel down Crawford Road late at night on occasion in hopes of encountering this "guardian" again. In one of our most recent ventures, I was approaching the bridge with my wife Linda in the passenger seat of my truck. I rolled my window down and slowed to take a picture of the eerie sight. As I leaned out of my window I heard some very loud, heavy footsteps quickly approaching the driver side door. I stepped on the gas, not knowing if it was a person and not wanting to find out at that particular moment. As I looked over at Linda, she too was startled—not because she heard the footsteps, but because she saw a large, dark figure moving past the rear window of my truck, completely blocking out the moonlight. Could we have finally had a close encounter with the guardian after all these years? I would like to think that is a possibility. There is also the possibility that it was a large person lurking in the dark woods in the middle of the night, but I think that may be creepier than the legend of the guardian.

Illustration of the horse-drawn carriage sinking into the Black Swamp, 2016.
Courtesy of Linda Cassada

Yorktown Naval Weapons Station

Traveling down Goosley Road toward the Yorktown Naval Weapons Station you will find Old Williamsburg Road. Long before the land was acquired by the Navy in 1918, Old Williamsburg Road ran through the weapons station connecting Yorktown to Williamsburg. This was a route heavily traveled by soldiers during the Revolutionary War and the Civil War. During colonial times, this little dirt road saw many horse-drawn carriages and stagecoaches transporting colonists to and from the capitol city. One such traveler was the daughter of Virginia Governor Edward Digges, only she never arrived at her destination. It is said that she and a few of her friends were in a stagecoach departing Yorktown after attending a party. A bad storm moved in while they were at the party and the coach driver could barely see the road through the pouring rain. Old Williamsburg Road was practically washed out where it rounded Black Swamp, but the horses clumped through the mud at an unsafe speed as the coach driver whipped and hollered, attempting to reach Williamsburg before the worst of the storm. With a crash of thunder and a streak of lightning the horses reared out of control and led the coach off the road, where it was swallowed by the Black Swamp. For the next several days search parties combed the swamp to no avail. No trace of the coach, horses, or the passengers was ever found. To this point much of this story is legend, but to many of the men and women who stand watch late at night at the weapons station, the residual of this tragic accident has called out to them like an echo from the past.

Today, the portion of Old Williamsburg Road where the coach met its demise is restricted by the gates of the Yorktown Naval Weapons Station. Late one night, a team of Marines was conducting a routine perimeter patrol in a HMMV. The Marines were driving down a back road through the woods when they came to a point where the road merged with another road. As they approached the merge, they heard what sounded like the neigh of a horse, along with the galloping of hooves and the clatter of wagon wheels. As they looked to the left, they saw a yellow horse-drawn coach approaching the merge. The Marines slammed on the brakes as the coach grazed the driver side front fender of the HMMV and continued on its path at full speed, disappearing around the bend. When the Marines searched for the source of the screams they faded off into the night without a trace. Many other

14

Marines and sailors standing late-night watch have also reported hearing the sounds of wagon wheels and horses accompanied by the dreadful screams of women.

The residual haunting of the old stagecoach is not the only anomaly manifesting on the weapons station. There have also been several reports of a shadow figure lurking around the barracks. One Marine woke up in the middle of the night, disturbed by a sound from outside his second-story window. As he approached his window, he saw the silhouette of a man crouched on the windowsill, peering in at him. The man had no facial features, just pure darkness where his face should have been. Letting out a startled scream, the Marine's roommate woke up and the figure faded before their eyes. The wall leading up to the windowsill was flat and brick; there was no way an average person would have been able to scale it, let alone balance on the tiny windowsill.

More reports of paranormal activity at the weapons station seem to center around a high-level security area. In the early '90s, Marines provided security in a series of watchtowers overlooking four quadrants. During the night and wee hours of the morning, they would hear footsteps walking up the spiral staircases to the towers and across the catwalks surrounding the towers. They could never seem to find the source of these footsteps, nor the answer to how they penetrated a secure area. They would also report hearing a "banshee cry" off in the woods while standing in the towers. Could this "banshee cry" be the screams of the young ladies meeting their untimely fate as their coach sank into the Black Swamp? Another interesting possibility is the guardian from Crawford Road. The guardian has been known to let out a shriek much like a banshee, as a warning to unwelcome visitors. Given the proximity of the weapons station to Crawford Road, there is the possibility that the guardian could be the source of these sounds. One thing is for certain: whether it's the guardian from Crawford Road or the old stagecoach and its passengers, Yorktown Naval Weapons Station is home to something unearthly, and to this day, the men and women posted there report hearing strange sounds and seeing unexplainable sights in the darkness.

Bellfield Plantation Site

Bordering the Yorktown Naval Weapons Station is the scenic York River. Stretched out alongside the York River you will find the Colonial Parkway, which connects the historic triangle of Yorktown, Williamsburg, and Jamestown. This route provides a picturesque view of the river as it winds down through the seemingly undisturbed forest of Yorktown. At certain points along the parkway little streams quietly pass under the road and flow on through the marsh, disappearing into the dense woods. One can only imagine that these were the very sights beheld by the first settlers to this land, still pure in their beauty and seemingly untouched by human hands. However, there was a time when these woods were home to colonial dwellings and plantations that have long since been reclaimed by nature. One such place is the site of Bellfield Plantation. The Bellfield Plantation has a long history dating to the early days of the colony.

Bellfield Plantation was built in the 1630s by early Virginia Governor Capt. John West. John West was born in 1590, to a prominent family in Hampshire, England. He graduated from Magdalen College before embarking on a voyage to the Colony of Virginia. He arrived on the beautiful shores of Virginia in 1618, aboard the *Bonny Bess*. One can only imagine the sights that lay before him as he gazed out over the young colony. The dense woods, tall grass, fresh air, and scenic shoreline had yet to be soiled by human hands. Shortly after his arrival, there was an Indian massacre near present-day Westover. West was one of seven leaders tasked with retaliating against the Native Americans. (Hatch, 1970, 11) Capt. John West survived the conflict, and in 1630, he built Bellfield Plantation along the river, on the outskirts of the village of Yorktown. Capt. West resided at Bellfield for nearly twenty years before the deed was passed to Edward Digges in 1650.

Son of Sir Dudley Digges, Edward became a prominent figure in Virginia history. Edward Digges became the governor of Virginia on March 31, 1655. It was during Digges' ownership of Bellfield that the plantation thrived. Edward Digges began growing some of the finest tobacco available at the time, and in 1664, he established E. D. Tobacco from the crop grown on the grounds of Bellfield. E. D. Tobacco was well received throughout the area due to its mild taste and fine aroma. (Hatch, 1970, 27)

Not only was Edward Digges successful in tobacco production, but he also became known as a "Silk Master" throughout the area. In 1656, he answered the Virginia Assembly's call to produce one hundred pounds of silk within a year. The methods of winding silk that he implemented and demonstrated to Virginians are still in use today.

Edward Digges died on March 15, 1675, and the plantation was passed down through his descendants. (Hatch, 1970, 34). In the middle of the eighteenth century, Bellfield Plantation was destroyed by a fire. The manor house that held such history and had seen such extravagance within its walls and throughout its fields burned to the ground, leaving only a foundation as a reminder of the once-thriving plantation house.

There is a mysterious beauty that is often beheld by old foundations of houses lying in the woods, seemingly forgotten by mankind. They cause us to wonder what once stood there and who inhabited the land. Once full of life and people conducting their daily routines and activities, they are now just vacant and abandoned. As you look at the shape of the foundation and the weeds growing up between the bricks, you can sometimes piece together in your mind an image of what once was. You can often feel the energy of the lives once lived there, energy that seems to linger on from years of events, happiness, laughter, pain, sorrow, and many other emotions once experienced between walls long since fallen. Such is the case with the Bellfield Plantation ruins. As you wander into the woods along the Colonial Parkway to this once-thriving plantation site, you will find what little remains of this previously magnificent structure. A few scattered remnants of what once was lie among the trees.

If you are driving down the parkway toward Williamsburg, you will pass a closed-off parking lot on the left. The parking lot has been closed since 9/11 as part of an agreement with the US Navy and the National Park Service to serve as an added buffer to the Yorktown Naval Weapons Station. You can obtain permission from the National Park Service to visit the site for various reasons. From the little parking lot is a path that leads back to the plantation site. Almost completely recovered by nature is the centuries-old brick foundation stretching out along the path. Just past the foundation is a little rusty wrought iron fence surrounding a family plot shrouded in tall grass and vines. This is the resting place of the prominent Virginia governor and tobacco farmer Edward Digges, along with his several descendants who inherited the land. Aside from these few visual reminders of what once was, could something else remain—something not as concrete, but more of a

Gravesite at Bellfield Plantation. Courtesy of the Library of Congress

spiritual nature? This is the question that three local teenagers set out to answer late one night.

It was early December, on a night so cold the chill pierced right through to their bones. John and Dave were two young Marines stationed at the weapons station, and Linda was a local to Yorktown. The three teenagers were driving around Yorktown when John informed them that he was a sensitive and could lead them to a place where they could find ghosts. Linda, now Lead Investigator for Virginia Paranormal Investigations, had always wanted to encounter something paranormal and jumped at the opportunity. John led them to the Colonial Parkway, which at night is a very eerie drive, as the surrounding beauty yields to the darkness. The car came upon the little parking lot near Bellfield Plantation when John directed Dave to stop the car. At the time the parking lot was not closed off as it is today. John exited the vehicle and led the group down a little dirt path into the woods. As they walked into the woods the darkness seemed to close in around them. They passed the foundation of the plantation house and continued to the little cemetery, the darkness of the surrounding

18

woods making it near impossible to see even a foot in front of them. When they reached the old wrought iron fence surrounding the graves Linda reached her hand through the fence. As she held her hand still, she felt a hot breath breaking the coldness of the night and laying upon her skin. Startled, she quickly retracted her hand. A mixture of excitement and panic rushed through her. Just then, what appeared to be two glowing red dots, almost in the form of red eyes, attracted their attention. The red eyes seemed to be watching them from out in the woods, taking the cloak of darkness as its cover yet unable to hide the chilling red glow. As the three stood there in silence, the red eyes disappeared behind a tree and reappeared a moment later. Questions and discomfort filled their minds. What could this be, and why was it observing their every move? Dave and Linda decided to head back to the car, but John wanted to further investigate the anomaly. As John walked toward the spot where they saw the red eyes the night grew still. The slight breeze that had been circling around them ceased. John continued closer and the night remained silent. The red eyes were no longer emerging from behind the tree where the teenagers first observed them. The absence of sounds in the night began to grow more deafening than a crowd of people, when suddenly the wall of silence was broken by heavy footsteps clomping toward John. He squinted into the darkness, hearing the voices of Dave and Linda, knowing that they were well off in the direction of the car. Suddenly the footsteps stopped and all was silent again, but only for a moment. Then, with a thrust to his back, John was suddenly swept off his feet and knocked face first into the ground. Shocked by the unseen attacker, John ran back to the car, where he was met by Linda and Dave. The three hastily jumped into the car and started down the Colonial Parkway back toward Yorktown. It was not until they reached the lights of Route 17 that the petrified silence was broken and the group discussed the turn of events that took place at the Bellfield Plantation ruins.

What was this unseen entity lurking in the darkness at Bellfield? Could it be Edward Digges calling out from beyond the grave? Does the ghost of Capt. John West still linger there? Or could there be an entity that has manifested to ward off unwanted visitors? Whatever it may be, the old foundation and little cemetery are not the only things left behind from Bellfield. An entity remains—an entity that does not want to be forgotten like the magnificence of this once-thriving plantation.

CHAPTER 4

Great Valley Road

Scenic Colonial Parkway enters Historic Yorktown at Ballard Street. As you approach this intersection, you will find yourself among the vast battlefields that surround the village. A cannon, perched atop a hill overlooking the trenches, serves as a reminder of the turmoil and havoc that war once inflicted upon this beautiful land. Fields torn and tattered by fighting men are now reclaimed by the face of nature, as acres of green now glisten in the sun. A stately brick sign with the top forming a bell arch greets tourists to the colonial city with the words "Historic Yorktown 1691." A left turn on Ballard Street will lead you down past the present-day courthouse and continue on to the beautiful setting of the scenic waterfront along the York River. Here people can enjoy walks along the river, a variety of restaurants, and a good history lesson from scattered signs along the way. During the summer months, the recreational appeal of these sandy shores draws in many tourists and locals alike. Summer enthusiasts enjoy jet skiing, sailing, and swimming in the waters of the York River, while its shores are full of people grilling, tossing around a football, and basking in the warm summer sun. You will also find a long pier stretching out into the river where sportsmen enjoy fishing and crabbing.

With all the fun and laughter taking place as you walk along Yorktown Beach beneath the beauty of a present summer day, it is sometimes difficult to imagine all of the history held by these shores and the significance they hold in establishing the village of Yorktown more than three hundred years ago.

Yorktown was established in 1691, by the colonial government of Virginia through the Act of Ports, which required people who owned land in the area suitable for town and port sites to sell fifty acres per landowner. The location proved to be a valuable asset for the purpose of collecting taxes for Great Britain on imports and exports. On October 10, 1691, Capt. Thomas Mountfort was tasked with surveying the land. (Hatch, 1973, 56) The current location was chosen and sectioned off into eighty-five half-acre plots in 1695. Colonists flocked to Yorktown with hopes of purchasing land in this soon-to-be-bustling portside town. In the next few years a church and a courthouse were built. (Trudell, 36) A carpenter

The entrance to Great Valley Road as seen from Main Street, 2016. Courtesy of Jeff Santos

by the name of Thomas Sessions purchased a lot along Main Street near the top of the Great Valley. The Great Valley was a natural wash cutting through the marl bluffs of Yorktown that provided the perfect road for merchants to carry imports from the ships at the waterfront to Main Street (National Park Service Sign, The Great Valley). At the waterfront end of the Great Valley, Thomas Sessions built a landing named Sessions Landing. In 1701, Robert Snead acquired the landing, building a store and storehouse. (Hatch, 1973, 158) This was one of many structures that attributed to the flourishing marketplace along the shores of Yorktown.

During the 1710s, activity along the waterfront greatly increased and would continue to rise over the next few decades. One factor that significantly contributed to this expansion was the exportation of tobacco. Yorktown's ports saw 32,000 pounds of tobacco exported annually. (Trudell, 47) Farmers soon discovered that tobacco took a harsh toll on the land. After seven years, the land was no longer able to be worked after the degradation of each year's produce. The wealthy plantation owners purchased more land for tobacco farming. The land was often large and distant from the plantations. This brought about labor issues, as the vast tobacco fields could no longer be farmed by a single family, leading to an increase in the slave trade. (Hume, 79)

Between 1698 and 1771, more than 31,000 Africans were brought into Yorktown. The Great Valley was the main road leading Africans from the ships on the York River to the market on Main Street. The Middle Passage refers to the route across the Atlantic Ocean where nearly twelve million slaves were transported between 1619 and 1860. During these harsh voyages two million slaves, whose names remain lost and unknown to the history books, perished due to the extreme conditions of the forced journey. During these treacherous forced migrations Africans faced severely inhumane treatment. Shackled in the bowels of rickety ships infested with disease and vermin, these men, women, and children survived several months without a glimpse of daylight. Many were chained together with such limited slack that they could not even stand. Dehydration, starvation, and disease claimed the lives of many Africans on these exasperating treks. To this day, deep beneath the Atlantic, trails of human bones line the paths taken by ships through the Middle Passage (National Park Service Sign, Middle Passage). The major port for ships transporting slaves was at the Yorktown waterfront. During the first decade of the eighteenth century, the passage led them to Barbados before arriving in Yorktown, usually during June or July. (Ivey, 55) African men, women, and children were led from the ships along the Great Valley Road. This road saw such pain, sorrow, and suffering as these Africans were forced up the road, still shackled together. Some of them were barely able to walk due to the lack of room to stand during their time barricaded on the ships. Their legs were weak from malnourishment and lack of movement, and some could no longer stand. As they fell to the ground, they had to be carried or dragged by those they were shackled to. The long line would continue up Main Street, being inhumanely beaten and herded along the path, knowing the fate that awaited them when they reached the top. Men were bought first, women second, children third, and the unhealthy last, knowing they would never again experience the liberty of freedom from which they were torn. (Ivey, 55)

The blood from thousands of Africans fell upon this road, where it would be remembered by the land as their names were lost to time. The strong, heartfelt pain and emotion has pressed between the pages of time several residual hauntings that linger in the Great Valley. Though some intelligent spirits may call out from beyond the curtain of night, many of the unusual sights and sounds experienced along this road are attributed to residual elements cast from the energy remembered by this blood-soaked soil.

During the day, the Great Valley Road appears to be a scenic little path that wanders through the bluffs from just behind Archer Cottage. To the left is a dense bamboo forest, and to the right ferns and tall grass sway in the breeze as it wraps around the mangled vines. As the curtain of night falls upon Great Valley Road it seems to come alive with activity from its dark past, as moments from its bustling days of roaring marketplace and busy ports play before your eyes and ears. Visitors to this road have reported hearing various unexplainable noises, including the cracking of whips, followed by the screaming of men mixed with the dragging of chains. Some claim to become overwhelmed with strong feelings of sorrow and hopelessness along this road. Are these reported occurrences only legend, or is there truth behind them? For a group of four local college students, the truth became far too evident.

After hearing about some haunted locations in Yorktown, four college students decided to go and experience the dark side of Yorktown for themselves. As they parked in the small parking lot near the mouth of Great Valley Road they were somewhat nervous, yet at the same time excited to journey into the historic town. They walked to a few locations along the waterfront before their fear left them and they grew more confident. They decided they were going to trek up to the Thomas Nelson House via Great Valley Road. As they came to the dark passageway through the cliffs, one of the two girls, Janet, stopped dead in her tracks. She felt overcome with emotion and sorrow. Janet never considered herself much of a sensitive person, but the energy emitting from this valley seemed to put up a solid wall that she was unable to penetrate without breaking down in tears. As the other female member of the group, Susan, tried to comfort Janet, she caught a glimpse of a figure passing through the entrance to the road. At this point Susan was more than happy to stay back with Janet as the two others, Dave and Peter, ventured up the dark road. As they walked deeper into the darkness the surrounding woods seemed to come alive with noises, most of which could be attributed to animals moving about and birds chirping. Suddenly the woods grew silent. In the distance they could hear something quickly approaching. The noise was unfamiliar at first, but as it drew closer, Dave identified it as the sound of wagon wheels on a rickety, wooden wagon. Peter, listening intently, agreed. The sound grew louder as they aimed their flashlights along the vacant road. At this point it sounded as if it was right in front of them, yet they saw nothing but darkness and trees. The sound of the old wagon wheels creaking along the uneven ground passed the two young men and continued down Great Valley Road. Dave and Peter rushed back to the girls and found them locked in a petrified embrace. When they asked the girls what was wrong, Susan broke the silence with a delayed answer. She told Dave and Peter how she was staring into the darkness of

24

the road when a wagon, seemingly out of control, came recklessly toward them. Within only a few feet of striking the girls the wagon disappeared into thin air. Could this wagon be a residual haunting of an old tobacco farmer, and if so, what fate did it meet as it rolled down Great Valley Road many years ago?

At night, the entrance to Great Valley Road seems to be one of the darkest sites in Yorktown. Not just because of the shadows of night cast by the tall trees that line the road, but due in part to a feeling that seems to overcome one as you stand at its mouth. It is almost certain that upon approach to Great Valley Road you will hear a few eerie sounds echoing through the night. Some may have a natural source, such as a bird calling from a tree, or a slight breeze wrapping around the bamboo trees causing them to meet with unnerving cracks. As you gaze down this dark road something seems to reach out of the darkness; not just one thing, but several. You may feel a strong urge to enter this road, yet a deep gut feeling that tells you to stay out. Could these feelings be due in part to prior knowledge of all that occurred along this road during its scuttling port days, or could they more so be brought on by the strong energy that still lingers behind? If you are feeling daring, why not see for yourself? But be careful as you call into the darkness, for you never know who or what might answer.

Beneath the steep marl bluffs of Yorktown's waterfront, along the York River, sits a quaint little cottage. More recently known as the fisherman's cottage, it is believed to be one of the houses of former Virginia Senator Thomas Archer.

This little house is shrouded in mystery. The Archer cottage is thought to have been built by either Abraham Archer or Thomas Archer Sr. sometime before 1750. The specific details are unclear. There is some history on the Archer family in Yorktown. Abraham Archer was an established merchant from 1729 until his death in 1752. Abraham left everything to his son, Thomas Archer, who worked as a surveyor from 1751 to 1754. Later on, in 1768, he became a ferry keeper. At this time, Thomas Archer ran a successful business and owned a schooner, which was later purchased by the state.

The exact construction date of the house is unknown, and very little is known about Thomas Archer. Through extensive research on Yorktown and all the founders of the village Thomas Archer is rarely mentioned, though he did have several dwellings throughout the town, and there are some documents that name him as the senator of the colony of Virginia around the turn of the nineteenth century.

Thomas Archer died in 1781, leaving behind his two sons, Thomas Archer Jr. and Abraham Archer II. Most of Thomas Archer's property was inherited by his son, Abraham.

During the siege of Yorktown, Abraham Archer II was captured by the British and held prisoner on board one of their ships. (Hatch, 1973, 123)

On March 3, 1814, a great fire swept through the village of Yorktown, destroying many of the old colonial structures. The fire is believed to have been started in an ordinary that sat up on the hill operated by Mrs. Gibbons. The devastating blaze consumed everything in its path, including prominent homes, small shops, warehouses, the courthouse, and the Parish Church of 1697. Robert Nelson wrote, "Almost all the houses on the water's edge are burnt also . . . I suppose there must be between twenty and thirty houses destroyed. How the houses on the left side of the street between the courthouse and my Aunt Nelson's escaped I cannot conceive." (www.DailyPress.com)

Robert Nelson's writings help to paint a picture of how catastrophic the vicious fire was as it claimed much of Yorktown. The Archer cottage was one of the many structures that fell victim to the fire, as the fire consumed all but

26

the foundation and brick chimney of the cottage. These remnants of the Archer cottage served as a reminder of that devastating day until the house was rebuilt in the 1820s. (Trudell, 71)

The Archer house sits along Water Street, at the entrance to Great Valley Road. During a typical day, Water Street is bustling with people as they stroll along the beach and stop in the restaurants. The Archer house, solemn and solitary, overlooks the beachgoer traffic.

However, is this cottage, seemingly frozen in time, the only reminder of days gone by? Or could some former residents still linger behind as well?

At night, the Archer House is still a picturesque little cottage. The bluffs set the backdrop for the cottage when viewing it from the beach. A street lamp along Water Street sheds light on the face of the cottage, casting shadows throughout the front yard and surrounding area. The left side of the house looks toward Cornwallis Cave, which extends into the face of the marl bluffs.

Everything seems calm and quiet as the silence fades to the sounds of the night. However, as some draw nearer to the Archer house, an unexplainable chill overcomes them and a strong urge to leave has been described by many. This could be due in part to the unknown woman who still resides at the small cottage. Many a passerby has caught a glimpse of this unknown specter as she peers down from a second story window.

One couple, Tom and Sara, were out for a late-night stroll along Yorktown Beach on a June night. They described the night as being very calm and still. A few couples and individuals passed them as they followed the sidewalk between the beach and Water Street. As they walked past the Archer house, Tom suggested they cross the street and take a look in Cornwallis Cave, which lies just past the cottage. Tom was familiar with the legends of the cave, but had never witnessed anything unusual there or anywhere else in Yorktown. Still, he liked to stare into the dark cave at every opportunity.

As they stood before the bluffs, movement attracted Sara's attention toward the Archer house. The movement was not that of an animal, nor of any other natural source. She described it as an illuminated orb traveling from the ground up and disappearing just before it caught her full sight. Sara, not entirely certain of what she saw, alerted Tom. The two decided to walk in the

Archer Cottage as seen just prior to National Park Service restoration.

direction of the Archer house and investigate further, hoping to determine the source of the paranormal light. Tom was fairly well versed in Yorktown legends and folklore, but he had never heard any claims of unusual activity in or around the Archer house.

Tom and Sara circled around the cottage and back to the Archer house historical sign. As Sara examined the sign Tom gazed over at the cottage. Suddenly, a woman appeared in the second story window on the far left. She had long, scraggly hair and appeared to be from a different era.

At first thought, Tom considered the house may contain an earthly resident who was just curious about the people trekking through her yard. Still startled, Tom stared in disbelief as the woman faded into the darkness— not turning, not taking any steps, just fading like a picture on a TV.

Just then Tom looked over toward Sara, who also stood staring at the house, frozen in shock. Sara's reaction confirmed what Tom saw and the unearthly origin of the unknown woman. Tom said that after the initial shock had diminished, the two of them hurried back to their car and discussed what they had seen with the doors locked.

They searched their minds, but were unable to reach a rational conclusion for what they had seen and how the woman had faded from sight. Tom could not believe that after hearing all of the legends, he finally had his own encounter with the paranormal in Yorktown and at a most unexpected location.

Virginia Paranormal Investigations's case files document at least three other sightings of this unknown phantom, as well as a medium review of the cottage.

Who is this mysterious woman that haunts the Archer house? Could she be a former license holder, previous resident, or maybe a townsperson who took shelter there during the siege of Yorktown?

Whomever she may be, witnesses to this day report seeing her staring back from that second story window, with a black, cold expression, then fading into the darkness.

Archer Cottage at night, present day, 2016. Courtesy of Jeff Santos

Cornwallis Cave during the day, 2015. Courtesy of Jeff Santos

Cornwallis Cave

Just behind and to the left of the Archer House you will find Cornwallis Cave. It is rumored that Lord Cornwallis established his headquarters in this cave near the end of the Siege of Yorktown. The most well-known legend among locals is that the cave connects to a tunnel that leads up to the Thomas Nelson House. According to this legend, when Lord Cornwallis had his headquarters at the Thomas Nelson house this tunnel was to be used as an emergency evacuation route. If the enemy closed in on him, he would exit through the tunnel, where a ship would await him in the York River, right outside the mouth of the cave.

Most believe that the cave was formed primarily by nature's hand. However, there is evidence to support the fact that man played a role in shaping it as well. (Hatch, 1973, 115) A man named Isaac Weld visited the cave around 1796, and stated:

> A cave is shewn here in the banks, described by the people as having been the place of headquarters during the siege, after the cannonade of the enemy became warm . . . But in reality, it was formed and hung with green baize for a lady, either the wife or acquaintance of an officer, who was terrified with the idea of remaining in the town, and died of fright after her removal down to the cave. (Hatch, 1973, 176)

In December 1848, Benson J. Losing visited Yorktown to conduct research for his *Pictorial Field-Book of the Revolution*. At this time the cave was secured by a locked door, and visitors were charged a Virginia ninepiece to enter. While investigating the cave, he met an old woman who claimed to have been a resident of Yorktown during the siege. She informed him that the cave was used by the townspeople to hide their valuables during the British occupation of the village. She told him there used to be another cave approximately a quarter of a mile down the shore where Gen. Cornwallis held secret meetings at the time of the siege, but no trace of this cave can be found. (Hatch, 1973, 179)

In 1862, the village of Yorktown once again fell under siege. During this time, Confederates and later Union forces occupied the colonial village. Beneath the bluffs a battery was constructed and artillery and troops filled the shoreline, ready to proceed into battle. The Union Army decided to use

32

the cave as a magazine, as it provided the perfect location to store munitions.

If you look to the right of the cave entrance, you can see square-shaped carvings in the face of the cliff. These squares supported large square pillars that were put in place to protect the entrance of the cave during its use as a magazine. Attached to this structure was a passageway, providing a secure means for the soldiers to transport ammo from the cave to the battery. (Hatch, 1973, 180)

There is no doubt Cornwallis Cave has seen its share of history. Many of the stories about this little excavation are speculation and still leave it shrouded in mystery. There is a lot of historical evidence to support many of the legends. With two sieges passing through this town, could a presence be left behind, still lingering in Cornwallis Cave?

Many late-night visitors to the cave will agree that there is an unearthly presence that remains. Some have heard voices that they believe are residual of the townspeople who took shelter in the cave during the Siege of Yorktown. Others believe the ghost of Lord Corwallis still haunts the cave, reliving his final moments before the surrender.

One may question why Lord Cornwallis's spirit would return to the cave when he did not die in Yorktown. However, it is believed that a person does not have to die at a location for their ghost to remain. Sometimes spirits are drawn to places where moments of strong emotion occurred. The energy from that strong emotion can burn the image into the atmosphere, allowing a window into the events when conditions are appropriate. This is most likely the case with the apparition of Cornwallis Cave. A second possibility is that an intelligent spirit can manifest at a location that held moments of strong emotions for them in life. One can only begin to imagine the emotion felt by Lord Cornwallis and the other soldiers during those final moments of the war as the mighty British Army neared defeat at the hands of the colonists. This emotion can definitely be attributed to some of the unusual occurrences at Cornwallis Cave and throughout Yorktown, not to mention the trying hours inflicted on the townspeople as they sought safety from the bombardment within the walls of the cave.

At night, Cornwallis Cave sits well-concealed by the eerie shadows of the vines and trees that grow about the bluffs. The glow of a street lamp lights

Cornwallis Cave with Confederate soldiers standing in front, 1869.
Courtesy of the Library of Congress

a historical tour sign just outside the cave and quickly fades along an old wooden fence leading up to the entrance.

The mouth of the cave is covered by a steel cage put in place for the protection of visitors and to keep out any unwanted intruders. The cage restricts one's full view inside the cave. The rear wall of the main chamber is visible, but another small chamber seems to veer off to the right.

Could this have been the evacuation route from the Thomas Nelson House?

The surf splash of the river meeting the sandy shores, along with a few other background sounds, can be heard from the mouth of the cave. A few of these noises seem to echo through the cave, sometimes emitting eerie sounds. But are all the sounds echoes of natural occurrences, or could some of them be echoes from the past?

One night in 2008, Jacob and his two friends decided to visit Cornwallis Cave to see if they could catch a glimpse of some paranormal activity. It was around one o'clock in the morning when Jacob and his two friends arrived in Yorktown. He had heard stories about some of the unusual occurrences that centered around the cave and wanted to experience them for himself.

The three guys parked in the parking lot on the other side of Archer house and began the short walk over to the bluffs. As they approached the cave everything seemed normal. It was just a typical summer night in Yorktown: very still, with an occasional light breeze sweeping in from the river. A few couples passed by, strolling along the beach, and their muffled voices could be heard from the cave.

Jacob began to snap several pictures through the cage covering the mouth of the cave but saw nothing unusual at first glance. When they arrived back at the car Jacob began to scroll through the pictures on his camera when something caught his eye. It appeared to be the right half of a person. The apparition was not clear enough to make out the attire. It faded out at the feet and above the shoulders, leaving no head in the image. The friends examined the photo and were in agreement about what the picture held.

Jacob scrolled forward to the next photo and saw nothing out of the ordinary. Whatever or whomever it was had disappeared within the few seconds between photos being snapped.

The story then gets a bit stranger.

After hearing about the evidence, I asked Jacob if I could see the picture. He then told me that he went back to his apartment and inserted the memory card into his computer. As he scrolled through the pictures the photo with the apparition was suddenly gone. The photo had been deleted and there was a gap in the number sequence of the photos.

Jacob was certain he did not delete it by accident and suggests the possibility of paranormal activity being responsible for the missing photo.

This is not the first time I have heard about pictures mysteriously disappearing from memory cards. This seems to be a fairly common report from paranormal investigators and residents at haunted locations. I have even experienced it myself at an investigation where the file containing the evidence was corrupted. A theory as to why this occurs is that sometimes ghosts may not want to be seen, so they tamper with the evidence, producing a corrupt or missing file. If this is the case, you should feel lucky that you caught a glimpse of something that many may never see.

Another theory is that the energy present when the photo is snapped may cause a malfunction in the camera. This is why a memory card may be corrupt, but it does not explain the image being there, then gone.

After hearing the story about Jacob's mysterious photo, I decided to venture out to the cave and see if I could capture some similar evidence of the supernatural presence.

It was early December on a particularly warm night when a medium and I, along with two other members of Virginia Paranormal Investigations, went out to investigate Cornwallis Cave.

We arrived on location just before midnight and started off with an EVP session. We laid down the voice recorder at the entrance to the cave and began to ask questions in hopes of capturing a response from beyond. After the EVP session we began taking pictures of the cave and surrounding area. Just then, the medium picked up on something.

She advised us to take a picture of the cave entrance. One of the investigators began to snap pictures in the direction of the cave. The medium claimed to see a mist-like entity fly into the cave and up through the top.

Mist at Cornwallis Cave, 2013. Courtesy of Roxanne Harris

Upon reviewing the pictures we could see a strange mist creeping into the photo, and a second picture revealed it moving farther into the cave. It should be noted that this was a particularly clear night with no fog or clouds visible.

The medium felt that the entity was protecting something of value, which I found interesting, due to the possibility that the townspeople were rumored to have hidden their valuables there during the siege.

Whether the mist was of natural or paranormal origin is difficult to say for certain. Though I have returned to the cave many times since, I have never been able to capture a similar photo.

To this day, locals and visitors alike report hearing strange noises emitting from Cornwallis Cave. Some report hearing male voices moaning, groaning, and even chanting. (Taylor, 2002)

Could these be the voices of British soldiers discussing battle plans, or could it be the voices of townspeople still echoing from a time long passed?

Another theory for the source of the voices points to more modern times. It is believed that before it was closed off by iron bars devil worshippers used to meet inside the cave and perform rituals. Some believe that these residual voices are remnants of cult activity. (Taylor, 2002)

Whatever the source of the sounds, it is most likely from another realm. The cave has been sealed off for years, so no earthly beings can get inside. One night, if you are feeling daring, perhaps you can take a stroll past the bluffs wherein lies the cave. But do not be alarmed by strange voices or eerie sights; they will only last a moment before fading into the night.

York River present day, with the mouth to the right, 2016. Courtesy of Jeff Santos

Ghost Ships of the York River

On a warm, summer day the York River is a very beautiful sight. The sounds of people swimming and voices from the beach seem to fade as one gazes out over the river's calm waters. A few sailboats pass by, adding to the picturesque view, and the sound of water splashing against the shores adds to the embrace.

As you sit on the shore and take in this scenic view, try to imagine this very river during the Siege of Yorktown. During this time these waters were full of British ships. Cannonballs pierced the river as the bombardment ensued from both the shores and the ships. The French navy formed a barricade from Cape Charles to Cape Henry, completely blocking access to the Chesapeake Bay. Several other French ships sailed up the York River in pursuit of the British fleet. As the bloody battle on the mainland soaked the ground the blood

Map of the Siege of Yorktown

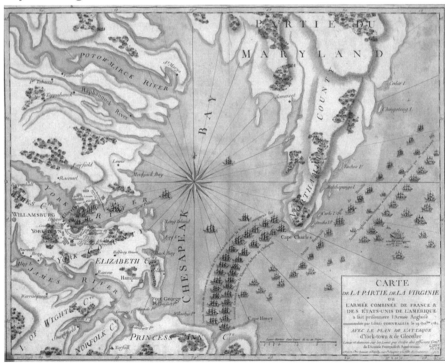

40

of sailors was spilled into the York River. Men gasped their last breath as the water rose over their descending ships, soon to be swallowed up by the deep waters. Meanwhile, British soldiers from the mainland attempted to flee the inevitable defeat offered at the sword of the Continental Army. Some British soldiers attempted to swim the width of the York River in a desperate attempt to reach Gloucester Point, where another part of the British Army was located. Even Lord Cornwallis ordered that little flat-bottomed boats be made ready so that he and his troops might escape to Gloucester. On the day that Lord Cornwallis attempted to lead this fleet of small boats across the river, the escape proved unsuccessful. The waters of the York River were angry that day, and the rough waters rendered the evacuation route impassable. Some of the boats were carried back to shore or were capsized by the decision of the river, while others were captured by the waiting French navy. Before the boats were captured, Lord Cornwallis ordered his men to throw all valuables overboard. Among the valuables, weapons, and soldiers plunging into the river was, as legend states, a large chest of treasure. It was tossed overboard from one of the small boats. (Smith, 20)

When the smoke cleared over the York River, several British ships were unaccounted for. It is believed today that approximately twenty-six British ships lay on the bed of the York River. Among the wreckage lies the chest of treasure tossed overboard by British soldiers. This chest has yet to be located.

A cannon recovered from one of the British ships sits on display down near Yorktown Beach. However, this old rusty cannon is not the only thing that remains from the British fleet. One late-night visitor to Yorktown Beach saw much more.

On a summer night around 11:30 p.m., Brian and his girlfriend, Cheryl, were strolling along Water Street. It was a warm night, not too humid, and the skies were perfectly clear as the moon, nearly full, hung lazily above. The couple decided to find a spot along the beach where they took in the night scene. They found a spot that seemed almost mid-beach. From where they sat, they had a good view of the Coleman Bridge as it stretched across the river, reflecting its vibrant lights in the water. There were a few other people scattered about the beach, and even one person who decided to take a late-night swim. As Brian and Cheryl talked time seemed to get away from them. Before long it was after midnight, and they found themselves the only people remaining on the beach. At this point the blue glow of the July moon drew their attention to the river as it seemed to radiate out across the dark waters. After a few moments staring off into the moonlight, Cheryl called Brian's attention to what appeared to be a very old schooner sailing up the river.

The *Alliance* and *Serenity*—colonial era schooners—are often seen sailing along the York River, as they offer rides to tourists and for special events. Considering the hour, Brian thought it was highly unlikely that either schooner would be out on the river.

The two watched as the ship drew closer. It moved without a sound, and seemingly without causing any turmoil in the water.

A ghost ship on the York River, 2016. Courtesy of Linda Cassada

42

As the ship came into the blue beams of the moon it appeared almost transparent. Just then, Brian's glance was drawn to a fog that was quickly moving in under the Coleman Bridge toward the vessel. The fog was unusual due to the clarity of the night and lack of humidity in the air.

As the fog met the ghostly vessel the ship was consumed, and both fog and vessel vanished into thin air.

Brian and Cheryl stared in disbelief over the sights they had just beheld. The couple has returned to Yorktown Beach several times since, but never again caught a glimpse of the ghost ship.

Another sighting of a ghost ship comes from Vivian, who works at a local establishment along Water Street. Late one night, as she was at the Duke of York Hotel, she noticed a fog moving in along the river. As Janice looked out at the river she noticed something unusual about the fog, as it seemed to contain within it the outline of a large schooner. As the fog rolled along the river the ghostly image seemed to fade. Janice was not sure if it was just how the fog appeared, or if she had actually seen a ship from the past still sailing along the river as a residual haunting.

The reason for the appearance of the ghost ship on the York River is no doubt due to the raging bombardment that occurred upon these waters during the Revolutionary War as Yorktown fell under siege. As mentioned earlier, moments of strong emotion, turmoil, and tragedy can cause a residual image to be burned into the atmosphere. War is one such scenario where emotions are so high, as men fear for their lives. Sudden death strikes throughout the battlefield, leaving images as stains upon the atmosphere which, when the conditions are right, appear to unsuspecting spectators.

Venture down to Yorktown Beach one night and pull up a blanket. Enjoy the scene of the river as the moon casts its radiant glow upon the waters, but do not be surprised if you catch a glimpse of the ghostly ship as it continues to embark on its last voyage.

The Victory Monument

A short walk up steep Comte de Grasse Street from Water Street will lead you to colonial Yorktown's Main Street. It is along this stretch where you will find several haunted locations and spirits wandering as you venture into the night and dare to explore the dark side of Yorktown.

Where Comte de Grasse Street meets Main Street, if you look to your left, you will find one of the most glorious sights and perhaps one of Yorktown's most well-known landmarks: the Victory Monument.

Representing the victory of the Continental Army over British forces, the Victory Monument extends ninety-eight feet, piercing the blue sky. High atop the monument stands Lady Liberty, with her arms outstretched as if to welcome the new freedoms won on these grounds by the blood of true patriots. The monument rests high on Yorktown's bluffs, overlooking the York River. A sidewalk leads up to the monument, and as you walk around its base, you will find plaques on all four sides, listing the names of French and American soldiers who made the ultimate sacrifice in contribution to the victory this monument symbolizes.

As you look toward the monument, the York River provides a scenic background as a few ships and sailboats pass by. It is a magnificent sight, and the meaning it holds draws many tourists and visitors to Yorktown.

The Victory Monument that we know today is the third monument constructed to commemorate the victory at Yorktown. The first monument was erected at the exact location of the British surrender as determined by William Nelson. Nelson indicated the original location with a stone cairn and four Poplar trees. A second monument was constructed sometime later and now lies forgotten in the woods of Yorktown. Our research has not provided the exact location of this monument. (Trudell, 151)

The first congress to meet after the victory at Yorktown passed a resolution on October 29, 1781, that determined a monument would be constructed. After one hundred years, a sum of $100,000 was devoted to erecting the Victory Monument that stands today on the bluffs above the York River nearly where the British surrendered. (Trudell, 152)

In 1880, one member of each house of the original thirteen colonies met to determine the appropriate location for the Victory Monument and to plan the Centennial Anniversary Celebration:

Victory Monument, 2016. Courtesy of Jeff Santos

Resolved, That . . . Congress . . . will cause to be erected at York, in Virginia, a marble column, adorned with emblems of the alliance between the United States and his Most Christian Majesty, and inscribed with a succinct narrative of the surrender of Earl Cornwallis to his excellency General George Washington . . . to his excellency the Count de Rochambeau . . .and his excellency the Count de Grasse . . . (National Park Service, Victory Monument Sign)

On July 7, 1881, the current location was chosen due to its scenic view. At the time, Confederate trenches and earthworks built by Gen. Magruder's troops tore through the soil. The government leveled the earthworks to lay the foundation of the Victory Monument.

On October 18, 1881, the four-day Centennial Celebration began with the laying of the monument's cornerstone. The Masonic Grand Master of Virginia, along with the Masonic Grand Masters of the thirteen original states, carried out the ceremony in which the cornerstone was laid. That day there were thousands in attendance, including many foreign dignitaries and President Chester Arthur.

During the four-day celebration, the US Marine band provided music conducted by John Philip Sousa, poetry was recited, and patriotic songs and hymns were sung. (Trudell, 153)

On July 29, 1942, the fourteen-foot-tall statue of Liberty, standing atop the Victory Monument, was struck by lightning. Lady Liberty was decapitated and her arms were destroyed as they came crashing to the ground with a thunderous sound that could be heard throughout the entire town. (National Park Service, Victory Monument Sign)

It was believed by many that this was a bad omen, as it happened in the midst of World War II. The damaged statue was replaced with a new one in 1957. Once again, in 1990, Lady Liberty was struck by lightning and replaced the same year. (www.VisitingYorktown.com) It is interesting to note that the second time Lady Liberty was struck by lightning was the same year as the start of Desert Storm.

As magnificent a sight that the Victory Monument provides during the day, at night it appears even more inspirational. Illuminated by four spotlights, the ninety-eight-foot monument towers in the darkness. The blanket of stars on the canvas of the night sky set the perfect backdrop for this symbol of victory. In the distance, the lights from Coleman Bridge can be seen as it stretches across the York River. Crickets and birds grace the surrounding tree line with their songs.

Looking up at Lady Liberty, with her arms outstretched, is a breathtaking sight as the light from the spotlights plays upon her confident stance. There is a peacefulness that surrounds you, a peacefulness that can only be attributed to the calmness after the storm.

After five years of battle that tore through Yorktown, victory was claimed, and the war was finally won by the patriots of this great country. This monument serves as a tribute to those who made the ultimate sacrifice and to the birth of a new nation.

In some cases, it is not a house or a building that is haunted, but the land itself. There have been several cases where a house was built on tainted soil and the residents have witnessed ghostly specters in the night.

Similar is the case with the Victory Monument. Though the Confederate trenches and bloodstained soil were leveled, the foundation that was laid upon them has not smothered the flame of the spirits that linger. Some who have passed by the Victory Monument at night have witnessed the paranormal activity that occurs on the sight.

One report I have collected is from a man who was vacationing in Yorktown with his family. It was not very late, merely 10:30 p.m. on a Thursday night. He, his wife, and two teenage sons decided to visit the town at night without the crowd of tourists. They figured they would make a short stop at the beach before returning to their hotel in Williamsburg. They turned off Ballard Street and on to Zweybrucken Road. Zweybrucken Road turns into Main Street at the corner where the Victory Monument stands. It was at this bend where the headlights from Dan's vehicle grazed over the tree line and illuminated what appeared to be four soldiers walking in formation. The soldiers carried their rifles with them as they marched from the tree line, visible from their feet up, and fading out just above the shoulders.

As Dan watched, the small formation faded out of sight as they passed in front of the Victory Monument. Dan and his wife looked at each other in disbelief. They decided to skip the beach that night and just head back to Williamsburg.

Another interesting anomaly often reported near the Victory Monument is the single ring of a bell heard echoing through the night. The source of the bell remains unfounded. It is not the same sound you may hear from a buoy out in the water, nor from a passing ship. The origin seems much closer to the monument itself. The reason for the sound of the bell remains a mystery, but some have suggested that the Masons would sometimes ring a bell at the start of a ceremony. If this is the case, then the bell could be an auditory residual haunting from the Victory Monument Centennial Ceremony.

One March night, I decided to visit the Victory Monument with Linda. We spent some time taking in the sight of the illuminated monument and its beautiful backdrop. We decided to walk a little farther down the sidewalk toward Tobacco Road and maybe conduct an EVP session. Just past the monument a bamboo forest grows on either side of the path. We have been near the bamboo forest in Yorktown several times at night, and I have to say, there are some strange sounds that emanate from its depths. Most can be attributed to the wind, as even the slightest breeze causes the bamboo to clack together. Also, there are a number of birds that nest in the woods, not to mention there are almost always deer in the area.

Yet what we observed that particular night was unlike anything we witnessed on previous visits to the area. From one side of the path came a single loud clack, then one clack from the other side almost in response. As we listened, the loud clacks seemed to answer each other from opposite sides of the path. Now, I have to mention that it was a particularly still night, and even when the wind blows through the bamboo several trees smack together. But this was only a single, loud clack. As we stood there in the darkness, our minds could only wonder about the possibility that we were hearing residual sound of ghostly soldiers signaling each other in the night as they would have more than 150 or maybe even 200-plus years ago.

It is an awesome thought to consider what may be lurking in the darkness. It is eerie at times, but fascinating at others. Could the apparitions of the men who fought for or against this nation still be wandering around the Victory Monument? Perhaps they are, still marching in formation, still preparing for battle, still signaling in the dark woods. Maybe Dan caught a glimpse into history, or maybe Linda and I heard a sound from the past. I also suggested the possibility that the source of the clacking may have been due to a bigfoot in Yorktown, but that may be slightly less plausible.

The Dudley Digges House during the day, 2016. Courtesy of Jeff Santos

Dudley Digges House

After leaving Victory Monument, let us venture down Yorktown's historic Main Street. As I mentioned in the last chapter, Main Street is the heart of our ghost tour. During the night many spirits, both seen and unseen, wander along this stretch of road. They linger in many of the colonial buildings and houses, some still going about their daily routines as if they were alive and others replaying their final moments before they gave up their ghosts.

I highly recommend a daytime visit to Yorktown's Main Street. A warm spring day in the village offers a very scenic and historic walk with a few scattered tourists along the way. Some of the locations offer guided tours inside establishments, while others can only be seen from the outside. Each colonial dwelling and establishment along Main Street provides a historical sight displaying old pictures and a brief history of each location. A few cannons along the street also add to the colonial atmosphere.

At night Yorktown's Main Street is equally beautiful, lined with old-fashioned street lamps that gently illuminate many of the historic homes and buildings. However, the entire feel of this location seems different at night. The serene beauty still exists, but it seems as though there is something more there with you. Perhaps the energy in the air is different, and perhaps this change in energy is emitted by the many spirits who come out to greet you as you dare to explore the dark side of Yorktown.

As you walk down Main Street from Victory Monument, the first house you will come to on the right is the Dudley Digges house. Built around 1760 by one of Virginia's first state councilmen, Dudley Digges, this dwelling is a fine example of a classic Tidewater, Virginia-style home. The house was built on land inherited from Dudley's father, Cole Digges. The Digges' family involvement in colonial government runs back to 1650, when Dudley's great grandfather, Edward Digges, first arrived from England.

In about 1728, Dudley Digges was born. When he reached his early twenties, Dudley became a lawyer in Yorktown. Dudley's first wife, Martha Armistead, met an untimely fate when she died giving birth to their second child.

From 1752, until the War for Independence began, Dudley was a member of the House of Burgesses. After his first wife's death, Dudley believed that her spirit lingered behind in their house. Some say he would talk to her during trying times, clinging to the belief that she was always by his side. (Behrend, 163)

Digges remained active in the Virginia Assembly until he was captured by the British on June 4, 1781. In that same year war ripped through Yorktown during the siege, and none of the homes or buildings along Main Street were safe as cannonballs bombarded the small town. As the smoke cleared, the Dudley Digges house was destroyed, along with many other dwellings. At this time Dudley decided to move to Williamsburg, Virginia, where he would spend his remaining years until passing away in 1790. (National Park Service Sign, Dudley Digges House)

But what about the spirit of Martha Armistead? Could she have remained in the war-torn house in Yorktown?

It is often speculated that spirits are not fond of change. There have been several cases where people have reported an increase in paranormal activity during renovations of their homes, businesses, and even during landscaping. Such is the case with the Dudley Digges house.

In 1960, Richard Marks was working on renovations in the Dudley Digges house when he encountered something from beyond the realm of the living. He wrote:

> While at work, we heard a woman's sobs coming from the bedroom. Her cries were so sad, they seemed to come from her soul. We ran to the room and found it empty, but a feeling of despair loomed inside. Later that day, we heard the moaning begin again. This time, we were positive someone was in the back bedroom. Instead of chagrining into the room like we did before, we decided to sneak up to the doorway and quietly peek inside. It was then that we saw a frightening sight! The floating apparition of a woman dressed in a blood-stained nightgown scared us out of our wits! The next day when I returned to work, I learned that John, who had been with me the day before, had quit and wouldn't be back.

To this day many have reported strange occurrences in the Dudley Digges house; it is said that Martha's spirit can still be seen at times floating above her death bed in her blood-soaked gown, unable to let go of those final moments when she drew her last breath. (Behrend, 164)

The Dudley Digges house is currently a private residence, so there may be little chance of a tourist to the city catching a glimpse of the haunting. However, when you pass by this residence at night, keep an eye out for any ghostly glow radiating from the upstairs window, as it may be the ghost of Mrs. Digges hovering over her bed, or even wandering about the halls, as Dudley believed to be a common occurrence.

Was the ghost of Martha Digges always there since her time of death? Could the renovations of 1960 stirred up energy that was previously at rest? Sometimes spirits emerge during renovations out of curiosity. They may be interested in seeing what changes are being made to their former homes. Others may not like the changes and may be appearing in protest. In the case of Martha Digges, it seems what Mr. Marks saw was a residual haunting. However, there may also be an intelligent haunting at the Digges house. Perhaps the same spirit that Dudley talked to on a daily basis is still there.

The William Nelson property, 2016. Courtesy of Jeff Santos

The William Nelson Property

As we move a little farther down Main Street, just past the Dudley Digges house on the right you will see the entrance to Great Valley Road as it meets Main Street. Next to this intersection you will find a plot of land once occupied by the William Nelson House.

The Nelsons were one of the most prominent families in Yorktown history. They had extensive land holdings and built many houses, warehouses, and wharves throughout Yorktown and its waterfront. "Scotch" Tom Nelson was the first Nelson to arrive in Yorktown. He was born on the Scottish border in Penrith, England. In 1705, Scotch Tom traveled to Yorktown and established the Nelson family in the small village. Scotch Tom married Margaret Read and had two sons and a daughter. His son, Thomas, went on to become secretary of state, while his brother William became president to the council. Both sons were significant figures in colonial era Yorktown.

Born in 1711, William Nelson was the eldest son of Scotch Tom. William Nelson received his education in England before returning to Yorktown. Upon returning William worked in the family mercantile business.

In 1738, he married Elizabeth Carter Burwell, and was appointed Sheriff of York County. In 1742 and 1745, William Nelson held a seat in the House of Burgesses before being appointed to the council. William eventually went on to serve as president of the council, and was later referred to as "President Nelson." (Trudell, 107)

William Nelson inherited lot number 47 from his father, Scotch Tom, and built an extravagant H-shaped manor on the land later known as President Nelson House. He resided in this distinguished mansion until his death in 1772.

William Nelson's house remained towering above the bluffs of Yorktown until meeting its demise in 1814, when the great fire raged through Yorktown and engulfed the prominent structure.

Now, where the William Nelson house once stood, is only a vacant, emerald field. The field extends from Main Street to the edge of the bluffs overlooking the York River. The field is lined with trees, with Great Valley Road to one side of it. A steep ledge separated the field from the street, and just over the hedge you will find a historical sign that details a brief history of the property. Two benches that sit in the field over near the bluffs provide a beautiful place to rest as you gaze out over scenic York River. This spot also provides a great view of Coleman Bridge.

William Nelson painting. Courtesy of emuseum.history.org

Standing in the midst of the field on a beautiful sunny day, it can be hard for one to conceive of the bloodshed that once soaked its grounds. During the Siege of Yorktown, Cornwallis and his men seized several homes throughout the small village for use by the British Army. One such house confiscated was that of President William Nelson.

Meanwhile, as the British were occupying the town and ravaging homes, Gen. George Washington and his men were preparing, surrounding the town and digging into trenches on the outskirts. The British were unaware of the impending attack by the patriot army of the Potomac.

Legend has it that a group of British soldiers were sitting around a table in the William Nelson house, enjoying a game of cards, when suddenly the silence was shattered by a cannonball that blasted through a window and decapitated one of the British soldiers. The others stared in shock as a rain of patriot cannonballs snapped them back into realization of the impending bombardment. The prominent house was pierced several times as artillery fire tore through the roof and the walls, killing every British soldier that occupied the house. During this bombardment several other homes and structures were destroyed as civilians and soldiers alike fell to their deaths.

It is no wonder the emotion and fear that those men experienced stained the land for years to come. To this day, visitors to the William Nelson property report experiencing strange occurrences. When night falls upon the William Nelson property strange sights and sounds have been known to emerge from the darkness. People have reported seeing figures moving about the field at night, frantically seeking cover from the impending bombardment. Men in British uniforms have been seen ducking behind trees, attempting to take cover from incoming artillery fire. The fear these men experienced in their final moments has been engraved in the atmosphere, replaying the images of terror as they met their sudden doom. (Behrend, 161)

People have also reported hearing men yelling and screaming, along with the sounds of cannons in the distance when passing by this field at night.

Just as the William Nelson house bore the scars of the bombardment until being completely destroyed in the great fire, the land still bears the scars today, although the scars upon the land can only be experienced on a spiritual level by unsuspecting passersby who happen to catch a glimpse into history as events from that fateful moment unfold in the night.

The Thomas Nelson house during the day, 2016. Courtesy of Jeff Santos

Thomas Nelson House

Directly across Main Street from the William Nelson house sits the former home of Thomas Nelson Jr. This Georgian-style structure is perhaps the most well-known house in historic Yorktown and serves as another significant landmark for the village.

The Thomas Nelson house is a spectacular sight during the day, as its elegant brick work and two chimneys tower into the blue sky. The sight, which is so arresting, is a very popular tourist attraction in the colonial city.

Known today as the Thomas Nelson house, the colonial dwelling occupying lot number 52 in Yorktown was built by Scotch Tom around 1730. (www.NPS.gov) There is some theory that construction of the home began as far back as 1711. (Trudell, 106) It is believed the bricks used in its construction were imported from England aboard Nelson's ships.

Scotch Tom died in 1745, leaving behind his widow, Frances Tucker, who resided at the Nelson house until 1766. At this time, Frances died, and grandson Thomas Nelson Jr. inherited the house.

Thomas Nelson Jr. was born in December 1738, and was the eldest son of William Nelson. The suffix Junior was added to his name to distinguish him from his uncle, Secretary Thomas Nelson. Thomas Nelson Jr. went to England to attend school, returning to Yorktown in 1761. Shortly after, he married Lucy Grymes. Thomas and Lucy entertained many significant figures at the Nelson house.

Thomas Nelson Jr. was a true patriot, and one of the many heroes of the American Revolution. He was a member of the continental congress and also served as general of the Virginia militia during the war.

In 1776, Nelson proposed a resolution to call upon the Continental Congress at Philadelphia to declare that they award freedom and independence to the colonies, and from this emerged the Declaration of Independence, which found Thomas Nelson Jr. as one of its signers. (Trudell, 108)

One very patriotic and selfless act of Thomas Nelson Jr. came during the bombardment of Yorktown on October 9, 1781. Gen. Nelson determined that Lord Cornwallis may have established his headquarters in the Thomas Nelson house. Without concern for his own interests and his magnificent home that had seen previous generations of Nelsons, Gen. Nelson directed artillery at his own house.

High above the bluffs of Yorktown, a rain of cannonballs tore through the prominent home that was, at the time, hosting Lord Cornwallis's headquarters.

58

According to legend, one of the cannon balls ripped through a dining room panel that concealed a secret staircase leading to a garret. It is said that a British soldier had been cowering behind this panel and was killed by the explosion.

The Nelson family contributed greatly to the cause of the American Revolution. Prior to the war they were a very wealthy family. Thomas Nelson Jr. not only contributed large sums of money to the cause, but also devoted his service to the Continental Army. Many wealthy colonists were hesitant to contribute, due to being repaid in Continental script, which seemed to them worthless at the time. Nelson even went as far as to take out personal loans in his own name to contribute to the colonial government's cause. After the war Gen. Nelson still held a lot of land, but he owed a lot of money as well. (Trudell, 109)

The Thomas Nelson house once again became occupied by soldiers during the Civil War. The house was used as a Confederate hospital, then as a Union hospital. (www.nps.gov) One can only imagine the deaths of countless men within the walls of this large house. During the Civil War field hospitals such as this had a reputation for using crude methods. Limbs were severed and tossed into piles in a corner, or outside a window. The incoming soldiers were triaged, with those who received minor injuries on the first floor, amputees on the second, and those with little hope for survival laid in the attic to die. (Asfar, 80) Imagine the agonizing screams of war-torn soldiers bellowing through the hallways and the smell of death in the air as amputated limbs and corpses fell into decay. Locations like this, where so many lives ended, often generate energy that stains the atmosphere as blood stained the old wooden floorboards.

The Nelson family retained ownership of the Thomas Nelson house after the Civil War until Joseph Bryan of Richmond purchased the property in 1907. Soon after, the home was sold to Capt. George Preston Blow of LaSalle, Illinois, who partially restored the property and named the property "York Hall." The National Park Service obtained the Nelson House in 1968, and completed restorations, returning it to its colonial grandeur. (Trudell, 110)

To this day, a cannonball can be found in the eastern wall as a reminder of the fateful battle that ensued there as Yorktown fell under siege. Various sources contradict the origin of the cannonball, as some say it was placed there during restoration and others claim it has remained there since that fateful day when Gen. Nelson directed artillery fire upon the grand structure. (Dupont Lee, 64)

The dining room in the Thomas Nelson house, showing the panels that conceal a hidden staircase. Courtesy of the Library of Congress

60

Aside from being perhaps the most prominent house in Yorktown, the Thomas Nelson house provides a very hauntingly beautiful scene as night closes upon it. A street lamp on the corner of Main Street and Nelson Street casts a yellow glow that illuminates the short brick wall surrounding the grotus of the Nelson house. A spotlight in the front yard shines brightly upon the face of the house, highlighting the beautifully laid brick work. Shadows fall around the pediment and windows, adding to the chilling appeal. Just above the cornice, the light yields to the darkness of the roof when it is soon met by the radiant glow of the moon sitting just beyond the northwest side of the house. The two chimneys extend from the ridge of the roof, with slight contrast to the dark blue sky and few scattered stars.

Though the Nelson house is a spectacular sight at night, there is still something that inflicts an uneasy feeling as you approach it. This could be due to the spirits left behind from its tragic and glorious history.

Until 1907, the paranormal occurrences in the Nelson house were experienced by few other than the Nelson family. With future residents and the home eventually being opened to the public in 1968, many of the rumored hauntings were confirmed as more and more visitors experienced the activity. (Asfar, 83)

Mrs. Blow recalled her experience while hosting a tea for the Garden Club of Virginia at the Nelson house. One Mrs. Chewning, who was in attendance at the tea, writes: "I asked Mrs. Blow if the house was haunted. She said that when they bought it, it was said to be haunted by a British soldier who had been killed in the secret stairway when General Nelson turned the guns on his own house." She went on to state:

> Mrs. Blow told me she had several ladies to luncheon a short time before, and one of them, much interested in ghosts, asked concerning the story of the British soldier and the panel. Mrs. Blow admitted that story was told of York Hall, but said throughout their stay, nothing had been seen or heard. No sooner had Mrs. Blow ceased talking than the secret door burst open with terrific force, knocking with such violence against the sideboard that several dishes crashed to the floor, shattered beyond repair! Absolute silence ensued. The faces of the guests blanched! Mrs. Blow, with admirable presence of mind, attributed the catastrophe to a sudden draught from above, and skillfully turned the conversation to other channels."

A Revolutionary War cannonball in the wall of the Thomas Nelson house, 2016.
Courtesy of Jeff Santos

62

However, Mrs. Blow also stated to Mrs. Chewning that there had been "no draught whatsoever; no normal explanation of the opening of the door possible."

Between 1907, when the house was sold out for the Nelson family, and 1968, when the National Park Service purchased the historic home, residents and visitors of the Nelson house reported several strange encounters such as the story told by Mrs. Blow to Mrs. Chewning. The attic was known to be a place to stay away from. Those who entered would often become overwhelmed with odors of stale blood and decay. Moans would be heard emanating from the attic and echoing throughout the hallways. Visitors also reported getting strange, eerie chills—enough to make their hair stand on end. Gusts of cold air would come sweeping through the rooms on hot summer days when the windows and doors were closed.

Now that the National Park Service owns this historic landmark, there is little opportunity to encounter spirits in the middle of the night. To this day, some who enter the attic claim to see, hear, and smell strange things. Some who have stood outside the Thomas Nelson house at night have seen a clearly lifeless Confederate soldier peering down from the attic window, his face covered in blood. Visitors to this house at night claim to get an intense feeling that they are being watched as they pass by. (Asfar, 85)

It is no question that many of the spirits that haunt the Thomas Nelson house are those of Civil War soldiers who spent their final agonizing moments within its walls.

In all of my investigations, the locations I have believed to be some of the most haunted were old hospitals. The pain and turmoil that was endured at such locations, along with the immense loss of life, has often left spirits lingering behind. Some of these spirits, shell-shocked and delirious in their final moments, remain troubled as spirits, perhaps lost and confused, wandering aimlessly for years to come.

The Nelson house is one location that has seen wars and years of tragedy, history, and prominence. It is no wonder that this may be one of the most haunted houses in Yorktown.

Cole Digges House

Continuing along Main Street, at the intersection of Read Street on the right you will find the Cole Digges house, formerly known as the Thomas Pate House. Many locals and previous tourists to historic Yorktown may remember this colonial brick house as Carrot Tree Kitchens, which operated out of this location for eleven years. Carrot Tree Kitchens moved out of the Cole Digges house in December 2013, and the house remains the property of the National Park Service. (Dailypress.com)

In 1699, ferryman Thomas Pate acquired this lot after John Seaborn, the original owner, forfeited the title due to failure to build a structure on the land. The original provision of the sale was that the purchaser would give up the title if no structure was built on the property within a year.

The house that stands there today is believed to be the same house built by Thomas Pate. On December 24, 1703, Joan Lawson acquired the house. After nearly two years, on September 24, 1705, Lawson sold the house to John Martin, who resided there for nearly eight years. In January 1713, Martin sold the property to Cole Digges. The purchase included John Martin's store house that sat on the waterfront down at the end of Read Street. (Trudell, 73)

Cole Digges was born to Susan Cole Digges and Dudley Digges around 1691. It is believed he was born on the Edward Digges plantation in Bellfield.

Cole Digges inherited lot 76 after his mother's death in 1708. In the two years preceding his mother's death, Cole Digges established himself as a successful merchant in the small village of Yorktown. Cole Digges became a member of the governor's council in 1719. He went on to acquire much more land before his death in 1744. His third son, Dudley Digges, inherited lot 42, where the Cole Digges House sits. Dudley Digges retained ownership of the house until he sold it to Daniel Jameson in 1784. From 1925 to 1926, the Cole Digges house as it stands today was restored by its then-owner, Mrs. Carroll Paul from Michigan. (Trudell, 74)

Reports of ghostly sightings at the Cole Digges house come from the time frame it was used as Carrot Tree Kitchen. One of the waitresses reported seeing a man in colonial attire walking into the restaurant just before it closed for the evening. She considered him to be one of the historical interpreters, perhaps just stopping in to grab a bite to eat. She turned to grab a menu for the late visitor, but when she turned back toward the door, he was gone.

Colonial apparitions are not the only manifestations that have occurred at the Cole Digges house; there were also reports of unexplained noises. Guests and staff alike would often hear footsteps pacing back and forth with no known source. Chairs would often move as if someone were about to sit down. Dishes would be knocked off the counter by unseen hands.

Since Carrot Tree moved from the Cole Digges house reports of activity have decreased. Perhaps one day the building will be occupied by another business, or another resident, and reports of ghostly activity will once again begin to surface.

In April 2017, a work crew was conducting restorations of the Cole Digges house. One afternoon, one of the workers went down into the basement to get a tool box. As she walked down the basement stairs, she said she was hit with a wall of energy and had an overwhelming feeling that she should not continue into the basement. The hair stood up on her arms and chills ran down her spine, but she continued on her way to retrieve the toolbox.

When she reached the bottom of the stairs, she turned and stepped into the basement, where she came face-to-face with a transparent specter of a woman wearing a long, flowing nightgown. The apparition appeared to float as she came toward the worker. The woman turned and ran out of the basement, leaving the toolbox behind. Though shaken from the experience, she returned to work the following day and claimed that everything once again felt normal at the Cole Digges house.

The Cole Digges House during the day, 2016. Courtesy of Jeff Santos

Grace Episcopal Church, 2016. Courtesy of Jeff Santos

Grace Episcopal Church

After leaving the Cole Digges house, a little farther down Main Street you will come to the intersection of Church Street. If you make a right on to Church Street and look to the right you will see the long brick wall that surrounds the Grace Episcopal Church graveyard. This cemetery is the final resting place for many of Yorktown's founding fathers and many early patriots who offered great sacrifices in efforts to support the American Revolution. Among the graves in this quaint churchyard lie the bodies of six generations of Nelsons, including Scotch Tom Nelson, who established the Nelson family in Yorktown, and his prominent and patriotic grandson, Gen. Thomas Nelson Jr.

During the day this little churchyard is quite scenic, providing a somewhat hauntingly beautiful landscape at the top of the marl bluffs. A few trees throughout shade your walk through the churchyard as areas of blue show through in places where the branches open up to frame out the sky. On gentle spring days birds can be heard chirping and a few bees may hum along the paths. The Grace Episcopal Church yard provides a very peaceful resting place for such gallant men.

As you gaze upon the church itself, you can tell that it is somewhat ancient. This little church has endured years of war, fire, and devastation, only to be rebuilt as the religious foundation of this small town.

Formerly called the Old York-Hampton Church, the Grace Episcopal Church was built approximately six years after Yorktown was founded. As with other buildings throughout the town, early settlers used marl in the construction of the church. Though marl was used mostly for constructing foundations, Grace Episcopal Church is one of the few structures built entirely out of marl. A high marl bluff provides the perfect setting for this place of worship as it overlooks the York River below. (Trudell, 58)

It is believed that Queen Anne gave the silver communion service currently used by the church today to the Kiskiack church as a gift. It was made in 1649, and has the words "Hampton Parish in Yorke County, Virginia" engraved on it.

The first church at Yorke Parish (built in 1642) is no longer standing, but part of the foundation wall remains. Within this old foundation you can find a tombstone upon which is etched the name Major William

GEN. THOMAS NELSON Jr.
PATRIOT SOLDIER CHRISTIAN-GENTLEMAN
BORN DEC. 18 1738   DIED JAN 2 1789
MOVER OF THE RESOLUTION OF MAY 15, 1776
IN THE VIRGINIA CONVENTION
INSTRUCTING HER DELEGATES IN CONGRESS
TO MOVE THAT BODY TO DECLARE THE COLONIES
FREE AND INDEPENDENT STATES
SIGNER OF THE DECLARATION OF INDEPENDENCE
WAR GOVERNOR OF VIRGINIA
COMMANDER OF VIRGINIA'S FORCES

HE GAVE ALL FOR LIBERTY

Thomas Nelson grave at Grace Episcopal Church, 2016. Courtesy of Jeff Santos

Gooch, who died in 1655. This is the oldest tombstone in York County and among the oldest tombstones in the colony of Virginia.

According to local legend, Governor Alexander Spotswood is also buried in this area. This legend is improbable, but the location of his grave remains unknown. (Trudell, 59)

The people of Yorktown hold the church very near and dear to their hearts. They each contributed to the church and ensured it was maintained and furnished. Just as the people formed the state, they also formed the church. The York-Hampton Parish saw many just and righteous men at its pulpit, and the parish was a very desired position in the colony. (Trudell, 60)

The church saw many families and early Yorktown residents enter its doors before the Revolutionary War and the Siege of Yorktown in 1781. During this time British troops under Lord Cornwallis occupied the church. The interior of the church, including the furniture and pews contributed by the people, were torn apart and scrapped by the soldiers. The marl walls of the church were used as a powder magazine. Windows were shattered, and the church suffered damages "over 150 pounds." (Trudell, 61)

After war ravaged the church and the town, the parish was no longer a very sought-after position. The families that used to regularly attend sermons at the church no longer returned. Many other townspeople turned to other denominations before the church was afforded time to fully recover after the siege.

The church once again became struck with tragedy as the fire of 1814 swept through the town. As with many other homes and buildings, the church was also engulfed in fire, leaving it severely burned. After the fire, Bishop Moore held sermons in the courthouse and in the Nelson house, all the while holding on to hope that the parish may once again be restored to its previous splendor. This came true in 1848, when the church was rebuilt and named Grace Episcopal Church. The appearance that it presents today has remained since these renovations. (Trudell, 61)

During the Civil War, foreign occupation once again plagued the town as northern troops swept into Yorktown. The northern Army decided to use the Yorktown courthouse for a powder magazine.

70

They used Grace Episcopal Church as a hospital for war-torn soldiers and used the belfry of the church as a lookout post. During their occupation of the church the Union inflicted no serious damage upon the structure. Then, an explosion shook the whole town as the gunpowder-filled courthouse blew up, destroying the entire northwest end of the town. During this explosion, it is rumored that the original bell was blown out of the belfry and was severely cracked. The bell was recovered and can still be heard today as it faithfully rings for services at Grace Episcopal Church. (Trudell, 62)

Just as the faith of the townspeople, Grace Episcopal Church has more than withstood the test of time. Through many trials and tribulations, through war and fire, the church still stands high upon the bluffs over the York River.

It is no wonder that with all this church has endured, and all the hearts that have embraced it, that there may be something left behind. As you approach this church at night, you will find it has a very eerie beauty to it. Lights in front illuminate the face of the church as they fade into the darkness of the churchyard. The first time Linda and I visited the church was on a cold November night in 2009. Scott Forsythe had told me about some of the ghost stories and we had to see for ourselves. As I looked through the viewfinder of the camcorder, a fog rolled across the screen just above the cemetery wall. Startled at first, we were quickly able to rule out it being our breath. Just then, we saw movement in the cemetery. We watched, happy we were catching a glimpse of some colonial-era apparitions, when three young guys were exposed by the lamppost. We talked to them for a few minutes, discovering that they were also ghost hunters out looking for specters in the graveyard. They said that they heard some voices and were unable to locate the source. It is possible the voices were traveling from the beach below, though the waterfront seemed fairly vacant. After our conversation we walked off to the next location.

Reports of ghostly encounters in the Grace Episcopal cemetery are nothing new to the sacred ground. As far back as 1791, Samuel Hawkins wrote:

As I walked past the old churchyard yesterday morning, I witnessed the burial ceremony of a beloved citizen. I was uncertain of his identity, but the people in attendance were indeed upset over his passing. One of the women beside the grave fell to her knees with grief. I thought it proper to offer my condolences, so I approached the grave site. It was then I witnessed the mournful group, draped in odd black costumes, dissolve into thin air. I now realize that I witnessed a funeral from bygone days. (Behrend, 142)

There was another sighting of this mysterious funeral in August 1995, by Yorktown resident Gena Page, who was walking her dog near the churchyard. She described the same procession of events that Samuel Hawkins witnessed more than 200 years prior. No one knows whose funeral this was, but the spiritual energy of the mourners has been engraved upon the land and still seems to linger in the air.

Aside from the apparition of the colonial-era funeral, there has been some other strange activity in the churchyard at Grace Episcopal Church. In May 2014, I was wandering around Yorktown with three other members of Virginia Paranormal Investigations. We were going to some of the haunted locations as we often do. As we walked up Read Street from the waterfront, we passed the churchyard. We stopped at a break in the wall to take some pictures, in hopes of capturing some unexplained anomalies. One of our members decided to start the digital voice recorder and ask some questions. Everything seemed quiet and still, when suddenly, as we were looking down at a particular stone, a shadow passed over it as if someone were walking past. We quickly looked up but saw nothing. We turned on our flashlights and searched for a natural source for the movement we had just witnessed, to no avail. There were no other people or animals to be found in the area.

A few months later, I received a similar report of a shadow figure in the churchyard. Andy and his girlfriend visited the cemetery one summer night in hopes of a paranormal encounter, and they were not disappointed. As the couple entered the cemetery from Read Street, they wandered around reading some of the old stones. Andy suddenly got a feeling that he was being watched when a dark figure caught the corner of his eye. As

72

he looked to his left, he saw what appeared to be a person standing behind one of the gravestones. As they squinted into the dimly lit cemetery they could see the figure moving about, from one gravestone to the next. Then, to their amazement, the figure faded into thin air. Andy searched the area with his flashlight but found no trace of any other person.

Not only have there been ghostly sightings in the cemetery at Grace Episcopal Church, but there have also been paranormal encounters inside the church. Reportedly, a woman has been seen dressed in colonial attire kneeling in the church. Her sobs echo throughout the pews as she lingers in the back of the church, holding a lifeless baby. John Carrey recalls his experience with this ghostly woman:

> I went to the church to do some routine repairs. When I first walked in, I saw a beautiful young woman holding a lifeless child in her arms. She was sobbing uncontrollably. Her long skirt circled the ground around her. I didn't know what to do, so I stepped out for a moment to give her some privacy. When I came back in a minute later, she had vanished. There was no way she could have gotten out without passing me! (Behrend, 142)

Passers have also claimed to witness this specter from the outside while passing by the church. Some have described a woman clothed in a lacy, black dress with a veil over her face, holding a stillborn baby. She can sometimes be seen standing at the church window overlooking the graveyard.

As with the mysterious phantom funeral, no one seems to know who this woman was or why her spirit lingers in the church. Perhaps with all the history the land holds, and all the trying events this church has seen, some moments still replay as residual hauntings. So stay observant next time you pass Grace Episcopal Church and its graveyard, and you, too, may catch a glimpse of the mysterious spirits that wander throughout the headstones and linger in the church.

Old Medical Shop

When leaving Church Street, a right turn back on to Main Street will lead you to the last three points of interest on the Main Street portion of our ghost tour. On your right you will see a Revolutionary War-era cannon placed in the field, adding to the colonial semblance of the town. The first structure you will approach on the right is a humble, white, wooden house known as the Medical Shop.

Lot 30, where the medical shop sits, was one of the first patches of land purchased in 1691, shortly after Yorktown was established. John Rogers, the first owner of the lot, retained ownership until 1706, when Capt. Thomas Mountfort purchased the land.

In 1769, Dr. Corbin Griffin acquired the lot, which at the time included four buildings: the medical shop, a house, and two outbuildings. Dr. Griffin not only practiced medicine, but was also involved in politics. Being an avid patriot, Dr. Griffin served the Continental Army as a surgeon during the Revolutionary War. Dr. Griffin also held a position on the York County Committee of Safety, which was in part responsible for a tea party similar to the Boston Tea Party that took place in the York River in 1774.

During the Siege of Yorktown, Dr. Griffin was held on one of the British prison ships. The events of his capture are not clear. During Dr. Griffin's imprisonment Gen. Thomas Nelson wrote, "I must request that your Lordship will inform me of the Reason of Dr. Griffin's Confinement on Board of one of your Prison Ships." (Trudell, 126)

After the siege Dr. Griffin was released and remained in Yorktown. He later went on to serve as a member of the state senate.

In 1806, after Dr. Griffin went into politics, Lawrence Gibbons acquired the Yorktown Medical Shop. Only one year later the great fire consumed the medical shop, leaving only the foundations of the old brick chimney.

In 1935, the foundations were located and confirmed to be the remnants of the medical shop by the notes on Dr. Griffin's insurance records from 1796. The National Park Service reconstructed the building in 1936. (Trudell, 124)

One can only imagine how this quaint little shop may have appeared in colonial times. Though the structure of the building may look the same, imagine the shelves in this little shop stocked with ointments, liniments, and other medicines of the period. Then, after the Siege of Yorktown, as with many homes and businesses, the shop was emptied. Most likely the British soldiers took what they could use and destroyed the rest. It is no doubt this land has seen its share

The Medical Shop during the day, 2016. Courtesy of Jeff Santos

The Medical Shop with an orb in front, 2016. Courtesy of Linda Cassada

of history. The great fire that claimed the medical shop started right next door at the Gibbons' house, but now the shop sits along Yorktown's Main Street, rebuilt and no longer bearing the scars inflicted upon it in history's pages.

It is believed that before the medical shop was built an old tavern once occupied the land on Lot 30. Evidence of this was discovered by a former resident who lived in the medical shop in 1981. She conducted extensive research on the land after she began encountering paranormal activity on a regular basis in her home. L. B. Taylor Jr. writes about her experiences in *The Ghosts of Virginia, Volume II*. When she moved into the medical shop, she began noticing strange odors with no rational source. One of the odors smelled like resonil, a salve used on wounds in colonial times. This could very well be a residual odor from the old medical shop. Objects such as flower jars were hurled at her. The rocking chair would rock back and forth as if it were occupied, yet no one would be near it. Footsteps would be heard in the attic during the middle of the night and random cold spots would manifest.

The owner caught a glimpse of the specter one day when she looked in her mirror and saw a partial image of a man in colonial attire.

It was noted by the owner that the spirit also seemed to be very jealous. When the woman had a date, lights would often blow out, and her keys would be missing. On nights that she did leave the home, she would return to find the place turned upside down. She believed that at times the spirit would follow her and cause disturbances at other locations as well.

A medium was called in to conduct a seance. She determined the spirit to be that of Robert Queasly Baker, a barkeep who came to America more than 200 years before. The medium went on to tell the woman that she and Robert had been lovers in a past life during the eighteenth century, when he was a barkeep and she a barmaid. At the end of the seance the medium asked Robert to leave the house. Shortly afterward the front door slammed. Even though he left that night, it is believed that his departure was only temporary. The woman believes that the spirit of Robert will be with her for life. (Taylor, VII, 361)

It is always possible that Robert's ghost still haunts the medical shop to this day. Since no one currently resides at the medical shop, there is no telling what footsteps may still be heard in the dead of night, or what random cold spots might manifest throughout the shop.

Swan Tavern

In the early days of colonial America there were inns, ordinaries, and taverns scattered throughout the land. These establishments ranged from rustic log cabins out in the Indian territories to more hospitable taverns, such as Raleigh Tavern in Williamsburg.

In those days inns primarily served alcohol, ordinaries served food and offered little room for overnight visitors, and taverns offered a little bit of everything. Such establishments were often constructed along heavily traveled routes and stagecoach roads. Given the distance between settlements, visitors and travelers would often spend the night in taverns before returning to their plantations or traveling to the next destination. (Trudell, 95)

One such establishment is the Swan Tavern on Main Street, across the street from the old courthouse on a corner lot. Though the lot was obtained by Charles Hansford in 1691, he failed to build on it, and the property would change hands four more times before the building requirement was finally fulfilled. In 1719, Thomas Nelson and Joseph Walker acquired the lot, and by 1722, they had built the Swan Tavern. Thomas Nelson passed his portion of the Swan to his son, William Nelson. William Nelson obtained Walker's portion of the establishment, and the Swan was passed down to Gen. Thomas Nelson in March 1761.

The Swan Tavern provided hospitality and accommodations to visitors of Yorktown for 130 years. The location was perfect, being close to the capitol and in the center of a bustling port city. Nearly twenty years prior to the opening of the Raleigh Tavern, the Swan was providing entertainment, food, alcohol, and lodging to many of the port city's patrons. (www.nps.gov)

The Swan Tavern is a story and a half, with a full basement where wine, whiskey, and beer was stored. On the first floor was the tap room, typically the most visited room in the establishment. Guests seeking lodging would have to check in with the bartender in the taproom. This would give the bartender an opportunity to entice visitors into trying a beverage from the bar. There were four to eight beds in each of the rooms, and often during busy times guests would even sleep on the floor.

The menu at the Swan would consist of freshly killed local animals and seafood. A variety of fish was offered, along with vegetables grown in the tavern garden. (Trudell, 99)

The Swan Tavern also provided many forms of entertainment. Small plays were presented, fortune-tellers would offer readings, and art exhibitions, and even freak shows would draw in spectators. Out in the yard of the tavern, people would often stop to see a wrestling match or displays of strength. Cock fights often took place not far from the tavern. Guests would sit around the fire on cold winter days or stop in for some ice water in the heat of summer. Politics, slave trade, and issues of the time were often discussed by patrons at the Swan. The bulletin board at the Swan provided information on social events, ferry schedules, and rewards for runaway slaves. (Trudell, 101)

In the early days of the colony the latest news was hard to come by. Governor Sir William Berkeley was not in favor of a newspaper press in the colony of Virginia and the most recent news was often received by word-of-mouth. When the mail carrier came to town, he would often arrive at the Swan Tavern. The colonists would be gathered around the tavern and in the street in anticipation of his arrival. Not only did the postal carrier deliver the mail, he also told the people all about the news he had heard along his route. Then the colonists would return home and pass the news along to their neighbors. Often the latest news was a few days old.

The Swan Tavern was recognized by colonists and travelers via the wooden signboard that hung out in front over the street. Signs on establishments in those days often had an eye-catching picture carved on them that depicted the name of the owner or location. This tradition was passed down from English custom, due to the fact that many commoners were unable to read, and therefore would identify establishments by the picture. The taverns would each strive to present the most memorable sign so that it would easily stick in the minds of patrons. As with the Swan Tavern, there are no sign boards from colonial times remaining in the Tidewater area of Virginia. The tavern signs we see today in Yorktown and Williamsburg have been recreated from old prints or copied from sign boards in New England or England. (Trudell, 97)

The Swan Tavern also provided a meeting place for the Freemasons in Virginia. The Freemasons are a group that often piques the interest and curiosity of many. They have been shrouded in mystery, and are believed to hold many secrets passed down and guarded since the founding fathers. "The Lodge at Swan's Tavern, Yorktown, Virginia, was warranted on the 1st of August, 1755 with the number 205 . . ." This lodge remains a mystery, as no records can be found. It is believed that the lodge and all records were destroyed during the Revolutionary War. (www.nps.gov)

During the Civil War, the courthouse across the street from the Swan Tavern served the Union Army as a gun powder and ammunition storage area. In December 1863, the courthouse exploded, completely destroying the Swan Tavern. The Swan, which served Yorktown and its visitors for more than 130 years as the source for news of history-shaping events, entertainment for colonists, lodging for travelers, political discussions, and warm fires on cold nights was gone, along with its outbuildings. (Trudell, 104)

The empty lot that served as a reminder of what once was the bustling Swan Tavern sat for nearly ten years before being acquired by Samuel A. Brent in the mid-1870s. Sometime before 1880, the Brent Hotel was constructed on the lot. Like the Swan Tavern, the Brent Hotel provided lodging and entertainment to Yorktown patrons. The hotel was passed down to Brent's children after his death around 1889. The Brent Hotel occupied the lot until it caught fire in 1915. By the time the National Park Service acquired it, the lot was vacant. (www.nps.gov)

The National Park Service began archeological excavations on the site in 1933, uncovering the old brick foundations of the Swan Tavern and its outbuildings. By 1935, the Swan, its stable, kitchen, and smokehouse were reconstructed on their original foundations.

While excavations were being conducted on the foundation of the old stables human remains were discovered in a corner. The skeleton bore signs of a hasty burial, as if the perpetrator took the victim by surprise and quickly attempted to hide the evidence of his crime. The identity of the skeleton found in the shallow grave remains a mystery. (Trudell, 105)

It is possible that the spirit of whomever was placed in this shallow grave still haunts the grounds of the Swan Tavern. Thomas Buckner, a Union officer during the Civil War, wrote of his encounter with a mysterious cloaked figure while he was stationed in Yorktown at the old courthouse. Thomas said, "I saw someone lurking in the shadows of the old Swan Tavern. His identity was concealed by a long, velvet cloak. After being discovered, the man fled." Thomas and his soldiers attempted to follow the cloaked man, but he disappeared without a trace. After the courthouse blew up, Thomas and his soldiers once again caught a glimpse of the cloaked man. He wrote, "We saw the cloaked man walking among the charred ruins of the tavern. This time, to our amazement, he vanished before our eyes!"

Swan Tavern with a face peering out the window, 2016. Courtesy of Linda Cassada

There have been several other sightings of the cloaked man since Thomas Buckner first witnessed this strange specter. In 1978, a Yorktown resident saw the cloaked man lurking around the Swan Tavern. He moved about the outbuildings and disappeared behind the corner of the old stable. The woman thought he may have been a reenactor and informed the park staff. They told her that there should be no reenactors in that area at that time. (Behrend, 153)

The cloaked man is not the only specter that has been seen at the Swan Tavern. Local Yorktown resident Vivian was at York Hall for jury duty back when they still held court at that location. Her brother was a sheriff's deputy, so she was dismissed early. As Vivian stood outside the courthouse, talking with her brother and the sheriff at the time, she happened to look up at one of the second story windows of the Swan Tavern and saw a woman in a thin, white, flowing gown peering back at them. Vivian's brother saw her too and asked Vivian to confirm the ghostly woman's presence. Vivian asked him if the place was open, considering the possibility that it may be a living person. Her brother informed her that the Swan was closed. Vivian said, "We went to go down the steps to walk across the street and it was gone. It just went poof."

This occurred in the middle of the day, in broad daylight. Even though I have been by the Swan Tavern many times during the night in search of the specter, our most interesting picture of the Swan Tavern was taken during the day. It was early spring 2016, and I was walking through the colonial streets of Yorktown with Linda. We were taking pictures of the locations for inclusion in this haunted tour guide with little expectation of capturing any paranormal anomalies. We usually associate ghosts with the darkness of night. They are usually moving within the shadows or glowing in some distant windows, peering down on us from above.

The Swan Tavern has reminded us that ghosts can be present at any time, even in the noonday sun. We may be walking among spirits of the dead. As we left the old courthouse and began taking pictures of the Swan, everything seemed to indicate a peaceful, spring day in Yorktown. Little did we know that in the midst of that beautiful, sunny day, an apparition may have been enjoying the view as well from the tavern window. Upon review of our photos, we discovered an anomaly (see p 80). It appears that a spirit may have been enjoying the festivities in the old tavern. If you look closely at the photo, you can see what appears to be the face of a person lingering behind the glass.

The sighting by Vivian and her brother, along with the photo evidence we captured at the Swan Tavern, tell us that spirits can be seen during the day. We typically associate hauntings with nighttime, perhaps because it is quieter and easier to notice them, or maybe because darkness can appear more eerie. If you happen to be passing the Swan Tavern on a sunny afternoon, do not be surprised if you are joined by the spirit of a colonial patron from long ago.

The Courthouse sometime between 1861 and 1863, being used as munitions storage.

York Hall (Old Courthouse)

Next to the medical shop, on the corner of Main Street and Ballard Street, you will find York Hall—not to be confused with the Thomas Nelson Jr. house formerly called York Hall by Capt. Blow's family. The current building that stands on lot 24 was constructed in 1955, and served as the Yorktown courthouse until 1997, when a new, larger structure was built at 300 Ballard Street known as the York-Poquoson courthouse.

York Hall is the fourth courthouse to stand on this site. The first courthouse to occupy lot 24 was constructed in 1696. (www.visitingyorktown.com) Prior to the construction of Yorktown's first courthouse, this lot was designated for public use by the people of York County and court proceedings were somewhat unconventional. Court would be held at a plantation or another home that was rented out to public officials. The location would usually be a good distance from the heart of Yorktown, causing great inconvenience for the local colonists. To top it off, the public had to foot the bill for the entertainment of the officials. This was one of the issues that led to the revolt under Nathaniel Bacon known as Bacon's Rebellion. The King sent a commission to investigate the cause of the uprising. The commission recommended that the public no longer pay for "liquor drank by only members of committees."

Finally, in 1696, the Virginia Assembly enforced an act that led to the construction of the first courthouse. The assembly determined that court would be held in a regular manner in a courthouse that would be constructed on the corner of Ballard and Main Streets in Yorktown. This location would be much more convenient to the majority of York County residents and would eliminate the need for renting other locations outside town.

By 1730, the tobacco industry had expanded, causing an increase in port activity. More and more colonists came to live in Yorktown, establishing businesses, wharves, and warehouses. With the increasing population there came the demand for a larger courthouse. A new "most imposing" courthouse was constructed of brick, with stone floors imported from England and interior panel work.

During the Siege of Yorktown in 1781, British soldiers occupied the courthouse. As the bombardment ensued many homes and structures were torn apart by cannonballs. The courthouse survived without a single hole from the rain of artillery fire, but British soldiers destroyed the interior and smashed nearly all the windows.

84

After the British evacuated the courthouse, the French Army used it as a hospital for war-torn soldiers. Even after the surrender of Lord Cornwallis, the French Army continued to operate their hospital in the courthouse. The stench was unimaginable, and the gentlemen of the town dreaded going near it. Eventually, the sheriff and magistrates determined they needed a courthouse and the French Army would have to leave.

After the French left, the courthouse was restored and once again used for court proceedings. The courthouse stood in operation until the great fire swept through the town on March 3, 1814; the courthouse was completely destroyed. A publication in the March 9, 1814, edition of the *Richmond Enquirer* recalls some of the details of the great fire:

> Yesterday about 3 P.M. Mrs. Gibbons' house in this place took fire, and together with the county Court-house, the Church, the spacious dwelling of the late President Nelson, and the whole of the town below the hill, except Charlton's and Grant's houses, were consumed . . . (Trudell, 122)

In spring 1818, rebuilding of the courthouse began. The new courthouse would be a twenty-eight foot by forty-four foot two-story structure. During the Civil War Yorktown was once again occupied, this time by Union troops. The Union Army established a magazine inside the courthouse, storing cases of ammunition and gunpowder.

In December 1863, gunpowder and ammo were accidentally ignited, causing the courthouse to blow up. The explosion could be heard throughout the town as it echoed down the streets. Several other surrounding buildings were also destroyed in the disastrous explosion.

After the Civil War, the Reconstruction Period was long and hard on the South. The former Confederate states did not receive adequate help from the Union. The corner lot of Ballard Street and Main Street bore the scars of what once served as the county's courthouse. The charred remains stained the lot as a cold reminder of the Northern occupation during the second siege of Yorktown.

For ten years, Yorktown lacked a courthouse. Finally a bid was approved, and in February 1876, a new courthouse stood on the lot. The 1876 courthouse remained until 1955, when the current structure known as York Hall was built. (Trudell, 118)

York Hall now serves Yorktown as a welcome center for tourists. Inside you can also visit the gallery, which displays artwork for sale or for the admiration of visiting spectators.

You may wonder how a newer building such as York Hall could be haunted. Spirits are not always drawn to a particular building, but sometimes to the land a building occupies. Whether it is an event that happened in a structure that previously sat on the land before anything was even built upon it, spirits can linger behind. Such is the case with York Hall, as strange occurrences have been reported after hours, when the building is supposedly empty. One of the ladies who works in York Hall relayed the details of her frequent, chilling encounter.

The first time it happened she was alone in the building. She had stayed behind to complete some extra tasks for the next day's event. As she sat at her desk deep in thought, her concentration was broken by loud, pounding steps walking across the floor upstairs. At first she thought someone else may be in the building. She went up to investigate the footsteps but found no source for the noise. Just then, she heard the front door open and the sounds of heavy footsteps entering the building. She checked the door and it was locked, just as she remembered it to be. There was no way someone could have come in without a key.

On another occasion, the woman was sitting at her desk in the basement, again alone in the building. She heard the sound of the elevator coming to life and descending from one of the floors above. She stood and moved around her desk, then walked over to where she could see the elevator doors. The elevator rumbled to a halt and she nervously watched as the doors parted and slid open. The elevator was empty.

These phantom footsteps came to be a frequent event at York Hall, accompanied by doors opening and closing and the elevator ascending and descending the floors with no one there to push any of the buttons. But what could be the source of this activity? What entity may be left behind, moving about York Hall after hours?

Perhaps the spirit of a soldier who spent his final moments on those grounds when the courthouse served as a French hospital still haunts the hall. Or maybe it is the spirit of a Revolutionary War army doctor walking about the floors, tending to his patients long after the war has ended. No one knows for certain, but for some York Hall employees there is no doubt that an unseen entity traipses through the building after hours.

Masonic Lodge #205 in Yorktown, Virginia, 2016. Courtesy of Jeff Santos

CHAPTER 17

The Masonic Lodge

Along Ballard Street, just around the corner from the Swan Tavern, sits Masonic Lodge 205. As mentioned, the Masonic fraternity is steeped in mystery and history. Many of our nation's founding fathers, such as George Washington and Benjamin Franklin, were Masons. Other key figures from the Revolution, including Paul Revere and John Hancock, were also members of this historic fraternity.

The origin of the Masonic fraternity is unknown, though it is theorized that it first emerged during the Middle Ages. The Grand Lodge of England, consisting of four lodges in London, was established in 1717. From this point on more complete records were retained and the Masonic fraternity expanded into the American colonies. (www.msana.com)

In Yorktown, the Masonic lodge was established in 1755, and met in the upstairs level of the Swan Tavern. Much of this original Yorktown lodge remains shrouded in mystery, as it seems to have been excluded from many records and no roster of its members has been found. The Revolutionary War may have had an impact on the lodge and its unknown history, as some of its members may have remained loyal to the crown.

By 1818, the lodge meetings were being held in the old Yorktown courthouse. Over the next several years, the history of the lodge is once again unclear. (www.msana.com) In 1881, the Masonic Grand Master of Virginia, along with 983 Masons from the thirteen original colonies, conducted the ceremony for the laying of the cornerstone of Victory Monument in Yorktown. (Trudell, 153)

In 1924, Masonic Lodge number 353 was established on Church Street. In 1936, the lodge was moved to its current location on Ballard Street. The number was then changed to 205, the original number assigned to the Yorktown lodge in 1755. To this day the lodge still holds this number. (www.msana.com)

Many outsiders speculate as to what the Freemasons represent, and they wonder, with great imagination, what events unfold behind the walls of Masonic temples. However, there are a few facts that we know about this mysterious and often-controversial organization. We know that the Masonic fraternity is a very old organization, predating the birth of the United States by several hundred years. Many important figures held positions within the Masonic fraternity. Some of these members held key government roles as well. One member, John Marshall, was the chief justice who formed the Supreme Court into what it is today.

With all of these significant figures in the Masonic fraternity, many form theories pertaining to the Masons secretly running the US from behind the scenes.

88

Some believe that the Masons hold ancient secrets and guard them with their lives, passing these secrets down from brother to brother throughout time. If you ask the Freemasons, they will tell you that they are simply a fraternity for the betterment of men, "emphasizing personal study, self-improvement, and social betterment." (www.msana.com)

A Mason once told me that they have certain ways of identifying another brother. These methods are subtle enough to go unnoticed by the average stranger, but enough to be detected by a passing Mason. He denied holding any significant secrets within their temples. For those interested in becoming a Mason, I was told that you simply have to ask one.

In all of our visits to Yorktown, I have always wondered if there were any ghost stories associated with the Mason Lodge on Ballard Street. I, along with other members of Virginia Paranormal Investigations, have conducted some extensive research into the paranormal activity in Yorktown, but have never discovered anything about the lodge being haunted. I have been past it several times, and often I would get a strange feeling, as if something was drawing my attention to the lodge.

I recall one particular night when it was snowing. I decided it would be a good opportunity to visit Colonial Yorktown and take some winter pictures. I also wanted to see if any lingering entities would be more or less active in this type of weather. As we were driving up Ballard Street, I noticed a very scenic, snow-covered stretch of road just in front of the Masonic lodge. I stopped the truck and stepped out to capture a photo of the beautiful sight.

I have to tell you, I am not a medium by any means. I have gotten chills here and there, but any evidence I gather during an investigation usually comes from our equipment readings and recordings. As I moved to take the picture, something drew my attention to the lodge. I can't say that I saw any movement, but something told me to look. As I moved my glances from the snowy street toward the Masonic lodge, I had a very overwhelming feeling of being watched. I did not know if the building was occupied or not, but it certainly seemed closed. I tried to rationalize a reason for the feeling that overcame me, but I couldn't. I had no prior knowledge of any ghost sightings at this location, and there was no movement that drew my eyes in that direction. I just wrote it off as my mind playing tricks on me.

It is possible that the land is haunted by a spirit who lost its life there many years before the lodge was built, but I had no evidence and no reports to support this theory. My answer came nearly two years later in 2015, when I was contacted by someone who had attended several events at the Masonic lodge. This individual told me that he was there for an event one night with his father. The lodge was crowded with people moving about, the low chatter of voices, and music playing in the background. He was standing there, somewhat disinterested, when he noticed a man who looked very different than the rest of those attending the party. The man was standing alone, toward the back of the room, with a blank look on his face. He seemed to be dressed like he was from the 1930s or '40s, with a blazer and tie, along with a fedora-style hat.

The man, remaining unnoticed by seemingly everyone else, then turned and walked out of the room, disappearing from sight. Curious about the strange partygoer, the young man hurried across the room toward the door through which the man had exited. When he emerged from the room he looked both ways, but could find no trace of the man. There was no way out of the adjoining room except through the door the young man had just come through. The windows were all closed.

The young man went on to tell me that he was not the only one to see this 1930s-style man lingering in the back of the lodge. Apparently others have pursued the man into the adjoining room as well, only to find that the man had vanished into thin air.

I do not know if this fedora-donned specter is what gave me the feeling of being watched that snowy night. I posed the question about the land being haunted, but judging by this spirit's attire, he is more likely related to the Masonic lodge. The lodge at that location on Ballard Street was built in 1936, a time period that seems to correlate with the style of dress displayed by the apparition. This does not mean that this spirit lost his life at the Masonic lodge. Sometimes spirits are believed to return to places that hold significant meaning to them. Perhaps this man died years after the 1930s, but that decade and that specific location hold a special meaning or fond memories for him. Therefore, he appears there resembling himself as he appeared in the 1930s.

It is also possible that this is the spirit of a former Mason, lingering behind to keep a watchful eye on the fraternity and his former temple.

The Yorktown National Cemetery during the day, 2015. Courtesy of Jeff Santos

Yorktown National Cemetery

Across Cook Road from the intersection of Goosley Road you will find Yorktown National Cemetery.

According to the National Park Service, Yorktown National Cemetery was established shortly after the end of the Civil War in 1866. The cemetery sits among several Civil War battlefields used during the Peninsular Campaign. It was during this campaign in 1862, that Gen. George B. McClellan pushed his army toward the Confederate capital in Richmond in an attempt to bring the Confederacy to its knees. Soldiers who met their deaths on nearby battlefields such as White House Landing, King and Queen Courthouse, Cumberland Landing, West Point, and Warwick Courthouse were later relocated to this cemetery. Several of the soldiers admitted into the Yorktown National Cemetery maintain unknown identities.

Another significant event that occurred near this cemetery was the surrender of the British to Gen. Washington in 1781.

After the soldiers from nearby battlefields were admitted into the Yorktown National Cemetery, the number of graves totaled 2,204. Of all the burial sites, 747 are known and 146 are unknown. Most of the graves belong to Union soldiers, while ten are Confederate soldiers, and three graves belong to wives of soldiers. The US Army conducted an inspection of the cemetery in 1868, and reported the following information provided by the US National Park Service:

> The interments number 2,180 of which number 11 officers, 716 white soldiers, four sailors, six colored soldiers, and eight citizens are known and two officers, 1,422 white soldiers, five colored soldiers, and 6 citizens are unknown. Besides the burials at the cemetery, bodies were removed from Williamsburg in James City County, and altogether from twenty-seven different places in the surrounding country, within a distance of fifty miles.

The Yorktown National Cemetery is open daily for self-guided tours. During the day the cemetery offers a very peaceful, serene ambience. Row upon row of flat, white headstones display only a small portion of the lives lost during the Civil War. Similar national cemeteries lie all across Virginia, each similar in appearance, with a two-story cemetery caretaker's house at the front of the property and an outbuilding standing nearby that is thought to have been built for the purpose of housing lawn care equipment. Each is surrounded by a chest-high brick wall containing a wrought-iron gate granting visitors access to the cemetery, and high above each of them the old red, white, and blue gracefully blows in the breeze as a constant reminder of the Union that still holds. All of them reflect the tragic loss of life that claimed so many during a great war fought between Americans on American soil.

Another thing that Yorktown National Cemetery has in common with some of the other national cemeteries is that it is reportedly haunted. Several late-night travelers have reported seeing unexplained lights dancing about the cemetery. Some have described these lights as blue flashes. Others have described them as musket flashes.

One of these encounters with paranormal lights comes from Mike, who was driving in Yorktown with some friends, observing the battlefields late one night. As Mike recalls, it was a cool night in late October—too cool for many insects to be fluttering about. He was out ghost hunting with a few friends and decided that the Yorktown battlefields might be a good place to catch a glimpse of some ghostly apparitions.

They came down Goosley Road and turned left on Cook Road, headed toward the village of Yorktown. As they turned on to Cook Road, they determined that the area near the Yorktown National Cemetery parking lot may be a good location to pull over and observe. The friends sat there and watched the battlefields, talking and joking for quite some time before one of them saw something. One of the guys, Ryan, interrupted the leisurely conversation, asking if anyone saw a strange, blue light over by the cemetery.

At first he thought it may have been lightning, but it was much too low. Any fireflies were also out of the question, given the cool temperature and season. As the four guys sat there with their eyes on the cemetery several minutes passed. Suddenly, the darkness was pierced by another mysterious blue flash, seemingly reflected by a similar flash across the cemetery. Mike decided that he needed a closer look. Joined by his three friends, he approached the cemetery wall. They all waited for several minutes, but the blue flashes of light failed to manifest again. As they left Yorktown that night, the four friends searched their minds for a rational explanation for this display of flashes, but were unable to explain what they had witnessed.

There have been several other reports of mysterious lights at Yorktown National Cemetery, but one August night came a much more definite manifestation. This report comes from the lead researcher of Virginia Paranormal Investigations, Linda Cassada, who at the time had not yet joined the team. This encounter was one of the personal experiences that prompted her to join Virginia Paranormal Investigations and further explore supernatural occurrences.

Linda was born and raised in Yorktown, and the small riverside village had become her thinking spot over the years. Late one evening, after an argument with her then-boyfriend, Linda hopped in her car and set off toward Yorktown. She turned on to Cook Road from George Washington Memorial Highway and ventured down the road, which was consumed by the darkness of night. She passed a church and the high school she had attended, as well as a few homes, all illuminated by parking lot or porch lights. She then entered the darkest section of Cook Road, where a dense forest crept up to each side of the road. Despite the fifty-five-mile-per-hour speed limit, Linda slowed her car, knowing she would encounter a few deer feeding by the side of the road. Finally the forest gave way to battlefields, and on the right was Yorktown National Cemetery.

At first everything appeared normal. The brick wall at the front of the property was awash in shadows as usual. The caretaker's home stood behind the wall, with a grassy, gated driveway reaching to meet the edge of Cook Road.

As she approached the driveway, her headlights fell upon something out of place. Standing with arms at his sides at the end of the driveway was a man in a navy-blue coat with a single row of gold buttons down the front. He wore matching navy pants. Wrapped around the top of his head was some sort of white fabric that to Linda looked like a turban.

He appeared to be staring at her oncoming car.

She was startled at first, then wondered what someone was doing standing out there on the side of the dark road at night. In all the times she had driven down that road at night, she had never once seen someone standing or walking along that stretch of road. There was something else that struck her as odd as well, and that was the way the light from her headlights fell over the man. His clothing was visible, but somehow grayish and dull in appearance.

As soon as she had passed the stranger she glanced in her rearview mirror to get a second look, but the stranger had suddenly vanished. At the end of Cook Road she turned her car around and went back for a second look. The man was gone, and she knew then that he had never really been there.

94

Later that night, Linda called her father to tell him what she had seen. "You saw a soldier with a bandage around his head," her father told her. It suddenly dawned on her that he was right. Bandages in those days were far more bulky. She combed the internet for images of Civil War soldiers and discovered that the uniform she had seen was that of a Union infantryman.

This soldier, who had suffered a head wound in a nearby battle, now wanders along Cook Road, a reflection of his final moments.

Linda has returned to Yorktown National Cemetery several times since this incident, hoping to catch another glimpse of this phantom soldier, but to no avail. She has not since witnessed such a sight. An apparition that definite is not a common encounter, even for paranormal investigators such as Linda, who travel to purportedly haunted locations on a regular basis.

One may wonder why a cemetery would be haunted. Of course graveyards have that stigma attached to them. People often imagine ghosts lurking about cemeteries, peering from behind tombstones, and moaning in agony as they wander through such sacred grounds. There are some that suggest a lack of spirits actually in graveyards, as they prefer to haunt other locations, or people that they may be more fond of. I do believe that the spirit is drawn to the body for various reasons. Some spirits may attend their own funerals and decide to linger by their grave sites. Perhaps they remain in disbelief that their physical body is six feet underground, and others may be mourning their death. Many spirits may come to visit the headstones of friends or relatives, just as the living do.

There are a number of possible reasons that a spirit would be drawn to a graveyard. In the case of Yorktown National Cemetery, consider the fact that the bodies were relocated after death. These soldiers met their demise on the battlefield, fighting for their country and the principles they believed in. They fell with honor, and some may consider it an honor to remain on that battlefield. Moving a body after death can sometimes cause unrest. These spirits may appear as apparitions, or sometimes as small orbs and lights. The blue flashes of light witnessed by many at the cemetery may be these spirits attempting to manifest. No one can say for certain why spirits linger at Yorktown National Cemetery, but the reports of paranormal activity along Cook Road indicate that there is definitely something lingering behind.

CHAPTER 19

The Moore House

Just outside the village of Yorktown sits the historic Moore house. The land which the Moore house occupies is very beautiful, as it extends from the front walkway to the banks of the York River. This location is a must-see for any history buff, as one of the most significant events in our nation's history occurred within the walls of this house: the surrender negotiations of Lord Cornwallis to Gen. Washington.

Just inside the door is a hallway that extends to the rear of the home, and off to the right is a doorway that leads into the parlor where the negotiations were held. When we visited the Moore house, a park ranger was there to answer any questions and to present the history of the house. We were able to freely walk around and investigate the colonial dwelling ourselves. The Moore house was magnificently restored, with colonial décor and furnishings throughout that added to the ambience.

The location was originally called York Plantation by Governor John Harvey in the 1630s. Nearly one hundred years later, Lawrence Smith II established the 500-acre Temple farm on the site. Temple farm was handed down for three generations before being sold to Augustine Moore in 1760.

Augustine Moore was an apprentice of William Nelson at only fourteen years of age. His father passed in 1767, leaving him three plantations. In 1768, Moore acquired Temple farm, and established his home in the current dwelling, along with his wife and son. Moore continued to work for the Nelson family, and in 1773, assumed the position of partner of Thomas Nelson Jr. and Co.

When the British Army under the command of Gen. Cornwallis occupied Yorktown in 1781, several residents evacuated the area. Augustine Moore moved his family to Richmond to wait out the siege. Little did he know that his home would set the stage for events that would draw near the end of the Revolutionary War.

In the chill of a fall morning, at ten o'clock on October 17, 1781, a blanket of silence fell upon Yorktown. The sound of a drum echoed across the land as a British officer bearing a flag of truce emerged from the south. The artillery bombardment had ceased and muskets were hushed. This stillness was attributed to the realization beheld by Cornwallis of his impending defeat. The message he sent to Gen. Washington read, "Sir, I propose a cessation of hostilities for twenty-four hours, and that two officers may be appointed by each side, to meet

The Moore House as seen from the York River, 2016. Courtesy of Jeff Santos

at Mr. Moore's house, to settle terms for the surrender of the posts of York and Gloucester."

The Moore house provided a convenient location for both armies. It was somewhat of a neutral zone, and not within range of the war that tore through the port city, demolishing many of the other homes. The Moore House remained unharmed by the barrage of cannonballs.

Gen. Washington allowed two hours for Lord Cornwallis to agree to surrender. Messages were passed back and forth between Washington and Cornwallis. Then, on October 18, British officers Lt. Col. Thomas Dundas and Maj. Alexander Ross met with allied officers Lt. Col. John Laurens and Second Col. Viscount de Noailles at the Moore house. It was not yet midnight when negotiations were finished.

Lt. Col. John Laurens presented the rough draft to Gen. Washington. Gen. Washington revised the articles and sent them to Lord Cornwallis. The articles covered the care and treatment of prisoners of war, along with the surrender procedures. Gen. Washington determined that, "The same honors will be granted to the surrendering army as granted to the garrison of Charleston." The American garrison captured in Charleston in May 1780, was deprived of the honors of war, therefore neither would the British Army at Yorktown be granted those honors. The British Army at Yorktown would, ". . . march out . . . with shouldered arms, colors cased, and drums beating a British or German march. They are then to ground their arms and return to their encampment, where they will remain until they are dispatched to the places of their destination . . ." After the battle had devastated the port town, the fighting was finally over.

The Moore house left the hands of the Moore family in 1797, when it was acquired by Hugh Nelson, son of Thomas Nelson Jr.

In 1862, during the Peninsular Campaign of the Civil War, Yorktown was once again plagued by military action. The Moore house sat between the Confederate and Union lines, well within range of the conflict. Soldiers came into Yorktown and tore wood from the house, defacing the colonial structure.

The Moore house was restored by the National Park Service between 1931 and 1934, just in time to be dedicated on the 153rd anniversary of the victory at Yorktown. (www.nps.gov)

Of the many who fell during the Siege of Yorktown, not all casualties were soldiers. Often civilians would get caught up in the pursuing battle and meet

Incidents of the War.

MOORE HOUSE, YORKTOWN, VA.

May, 1862.

The Moore House during the Civil War. Courtesy of the Library of Congress

their demise. On October 13, 1781, John Turner's life was claimed by a stray bullet. John Turner was a local merchant in Yorktown who happened to be a spectator at the bombardment. As he watched the battle, he was pierced by a musket ball and rushed to the Moore house. His wife, Clara, frantically tended to her wounded husband while waiting for the doctor to arrive. Clara's attempt to treat John proved unsuccessful, as he died right there at the Moore house.

John Turner was buried in the small plot of the Moore property. His gravestone was found in the basement of the Moore house more than one hundred years later. It remains a mystery as to why Turner's gravestone was placed in the cellar, but it was eventually returned to the location believed to be his grave site. The engraving on his stone reads, "Ah cruel ball, so sudden to disarm, and tear my tender husband from my arms. How can I grieve too much, what time shall end, my mourning for so good, so kind, a friend."

John Turner grave site at the Moore house, 2016. Courtesy of Linda Cassada

100

These words reflect the heartfelt pain and sorrow Clara felt at the loss of her husband. It is said that she continued to blame herself and eventually died of a broken heart. It is this type of emotion that often leaves behind a mournful spirit. Such is the case with Clara Turner, as apparently her specter still roams the grounds of the Moore house. She wanders the empty halls and peers down from the second story window as if she is still eagerly awaiting the arrival of the doctor.

A local Yorktown resident saw her by the ledge of the York River one evening. Clara seemed as if she was contemplating suicide. She appeared to be very upset as she wiped her eyes with a handkerchief. Then lights from a passing car revealed her to be transparent, as they illuminated the trees behind her. (Behrend, 128). Other late-night visitors to the Moore house claim they have seen this mournful spirit moving about the cemetery and kneeling beside John Turner's grave. Perhaps this is the heartbroken spirit of Clara eternally mourning the loss of her husband.

Another interesting report I gathered about the Moore house cemetery comes from an employee at a local establishment in Yorktown. She said she has lived in Yorktown her entire life. When she was a teenager, she and her friends would often go out to the Moore house at night. One July night, while they were walking around the area, they saw some movement over by the small cemetery on the Moore house property. As they got closer, they saw three children dancing around in the cemetery. She shined her light on them and they vanished into thin air. No one seems to have any theories as to who these ghostly children are or why they gaily dance in the cemetery, but one thing is certain, there is definitely some unexplainable activity occurring throughout these historic grounds.

CHAPTER 20

Surrender Field

The morning of October 19, 1781, fifes emitting from the British camp at Yorktown pierced the silence. A feeling of victory and relief fell over the allied forces, as they knew these fifes signaled the surrender of the British Army. As the drummer beat on a drum shrouded in a black handkerchief, the defeated army of Lord Cornwallis marched out on to Surrender Field. The British soldiers were quite a sight to behold, as endless columns marched on to the field dressed in their sharpest uniforms. Some were in tears, distraught and weary, as they prepared to lay down their arms in defeat.

One can only imagine the emotion they felt and the thoughts that raced through their heads as they each laid down their muskets. Lord Cornwallis was nowhere to be found at the surrender. He claimed to be ill and stayed in his quarters back in Yorktown. As the surrender was underway, twenty-five ships bearing 7,000 British troops were being dispatched from New York, but the ships would arrive one week too late. Lord Cornwallis wrote to Gen. Sir Henry Clinton, "I have the mortification to inform your Excellency that I have been forced to give up the posts of Yorktown and Gloucester, and to surrender the troops under my command, by capitulation on the 19the instant, as prisoners of war to the combined forces of America and France."

More than 7,200 British soldiers were taken prisoner at Yorktown and sent off to prison camps in Virginia and Maryland. Allied forces also acquired thousands of muskets and 244 pieces of artillery from the British. Lord Cornwallis and his officers were granted parole and returned to New York.

Congress in Philadelphia was informed of the surrender on October 22, and the news quickly spread through the streets. The king did not learn about the surrender until November 25. The news surprised him, but he decided to continue the war. On November 30, 1782, the provisional articles were signed and nearly one year later, a treaty was finally signed officially ending the Revolutionary War. (www.visitingyorktown.com)

Today, Surrender Field is a beautiful sight. It sits along Surrender Road, surrounded by tall trees and forest. A split-rail fence lines the spot where the British ranks marched to lay down their arms. Toward the back of the field there is an overlook pavilion providing a scenic view of the field. The walkway leading up to the pavilion is lined with British artillery captured by the Continental Army at Yorktown. Inside the pavilion a historical sign presents

Surrender Field during the day, 2016. Courtesy of Jeff Santos

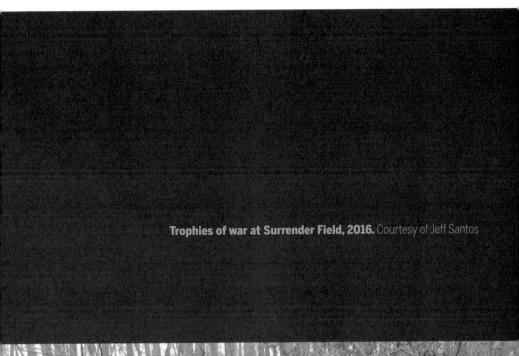

Trophies of war at Surrender Field, 2016. Courtesy of Jeff Santos

Light anomaly at Surrender Field, 2014. Courtesy of Linda Cassada

the events of the surrender. You can also push a button on the sign and hear a narration of that victorious day. Surrender Field is an awesome location to visit during the day, serving as a monument to a free and independent nation.

At night Surrender Road can be very eerie. There have been several strange anomalies witnessed in Surrender Field by those who have ventured down Surrender Road in the darkness. It is no wonder with all of the events that unfolded on Surrender Field that several entities may linger. People have reported seeing lights out on the field. Some have described them as flashes, while others have described them as a glare off of a shiny metallic surface. These lights have not only been seen at night, but also in the late evening, just as the sun is going down.

Linda was driving around Yorktown one evening, snapping pictures of the battlefields and other various locations, when she happened to notice a light anomaly in one of her pictures. The picture was taken in the area of Surrender Field where many report seeing strange lights. After noticing the anomaly she took several other pictures, but it failed to appear again.

Light anomalies have been reported throughout several other Yorktown battlefields. Some believe they are spirits of soldiers attempting to manifest. Another theory suggests these flashes are residuals of musket fire from the Revolutionary War. Some have even described the sounds of artillery fire and gunshots accompanying these flashes.

I would not doubt that these battlefields are haunted. The fighting these soldiers endured was more trying and emotionally draining than we could ever imagine. As they fought with muskets and swords, as artillery rounds tore through them, their blood soaked these battlefields. The blood was ingrained deep in the soil, and just as the land is soaked in their blood, these battlefields are soaked in their spirits. The spirits of brave men who gave all so that we can enjoy the liberties we have today. Tread lightly on these fields. They are sacred ground to us, our nation, and the spirits who linger among them. Watch closely as you pass, for you too may catch a glimpse of a war from long ago still being fought.

Paranormal Pit Stops

Before we depart from the colonial area of Yorktown, I woud like to talk about a few paranormal pit stops. Paranormal pit stop is a term I use to refer to any pit stops, such as restaurants, hotels, and stores, where you may encounter some paranormal activity. Such establishments can often be found in areas like Yorktown that have an extensive history and are steeped in hauntings.

Duke of York Hotel

Duke of York Hotel sits along Water Street, right across from Yorktown Beach and the York River. Several of the rooms provide a balcony that offers a picturesque, bird's-eye view of the river and the tourist area below. The inside of the hotel is very welcoming, with a relaxing atmosphere. While gathering information for this book, Linda and I had the opportunity to stop in the Duke of York Hotel and talk with some of the staff. I have to say that Manager Vivian Harris, along with the owner and other staff members we met, are very friendly—a good representation of the type of people you will meet when you visit Yorktown. For an overnight visit, I would highly recommend you check into the Duke of York Hotel for a dose of true southern hospitality.

During our conversation with Vivian, we talked about some of the history of Yorktown and what it was like living in such a quaint, colonial town. Our topic of conversation turned to ghost stories, and I asked Vivian if she ever had any strange encounters with paranormal entities while working at the Duke of York. Given its location along the river that once saw bustling ports, naval battles, and a war that ravaged the town, I figured it had to be haunted. Sure enough, Vivian had some personal encounters to share with us. She said, "It's mostly in the wintertime. You're the only person in the hotel. We have no guests, the restaurant is closed, and it's late at night. You can be sitting back here reading or on the computer and I have heard somebody talking down the hall." She wondered if someone had come in through the back door, or perhaps had come down from an upper floor on the elevator without her noticing. Vivian got up from behind the desk and went down the hall toward the voices but the chatter ceased. No one was there. Vivian continued, "I came back and about a half an hour later, somebody was having a conversation." Once again, no source was found. Vivian was unable to make out any of the words. She said the men were talking low, discussing something in mumbled voices. This was not the first time Vivian heard these phantom voices. She said it has happened to her several times.

The night shift employees have also had strange experiences in the hotel. They have heard someone walk up to the front desk, but when they went to tend to the customer no one was there.

The restaurant at the Duke of York Hotel is also reported to be haunted. The restaurant manager was cleaning up one night around 9:30 p.m., with only one customer remaining in the establishment. After the customer left she continued to clean up. The hallway in front of the restaurant is called the "tunnel," and there are a few tables and chairs by the glass windows at the front of the restaurant. She came out of the kitchen and noticed a man sitting at one of the tables. She informed him that they were closed and the man vanished into thin air.

The property on which the hotel sits has been in the Crocket family for more than one hundred years. The rear section of the hotel was constructed in 1964, while the front section that overlooks the river was constructed fifteen years later. Vivian pointed out the fact that there are battlefields all around the area. Perhaps some of these spirits may be lingering soldiers. Another theory is that they may be ancestors of Mr. Crocket, the hotel owner. Mr. Crocket did stop in while we were conducting the interview. He has not had any paranormal encounters at the hotel, but he had a wealth of insight into Yorktown's days gone by.

The Duke of York Hotel is at 508 Water Street in Yorktown. They have a website, www.DukeofYork.com, where you can make reservations and view pictures of the rooms.

The Yorktown Pub

The Yorktown Pub is a small, brick building with large windows along the front that sits farther down Water Street, just before Read Street. The establishment is a well-known landmark for friendly locals. During a visit to the restaurant for lunch, you may encounter York County Sheriff Danny Diggs and a few other deputies at a table enjoying their meal. At night, you are certain to meet many of the locals who frequent the restaurant for good drinks, appetizers, and music by local bands. I have had the opportunity to stop in at the Yorktown

Pub on a few occasions and can say that their pulled pork sandwiches are some of the best I have tasted in the area.

Not only does the Yorktown Pub offer great food and beer, but it is rumored to be haunted as well. On the hill behind the Yorktown Pub sits an old, wooden building—a long, narrow row of connected rooms that, according to legend, used to be a motel. Now the old building is used for storage, but perhaps something lingers behind from its days as a motel. There have been sightings of a figure standing in the doorway of one of the rooms. He appears transparent, then fades into the darkness. I first received this report from a local in 2013, and a similar occurrence was reported on a few other occasions. The pub also seems to have an entity. According to one of the staff members, they have witnessed some strange occurrences, usually at night, after the patrons have left and the business has closed. This employee mentioned that doors and cabinets will open and close, and items will get knocked off tables without reasonable explanation. No one quite knows who this unseen spirit is, but if you are in Yorktown, why not stop in the pub and have a spirit with a spirit?

The Yorktown Pub is open Sunday through Thursday from 11 a.m. to midnight and Friday and Saturday until 2 a.m.

Dollar General

Certainly Dollar General needs no introduction, as most readers may already know what type of store it is and what they sell. However, for those of you who have never visited one, it is a great place to find good deals on everything from food and snacks to décor and kitchen utensils, with a little bit of everything in between.

Along with great deals, the Dollar General in Yorktown may also offer a ghost. According to one of the store associates, unusual activity begins when the workday ends. When all of the customers have left for the day and they are closing the store, employees will often hear heavy footsteps walking through the store. When they go to find the source no one is there. Also, shopping carts are rumored to move by themselves, and the sound of them crashing together or into store displays is sometimes heard. The employee has also heard someone whistling in the store. Perhaps this is the ghost of an unhappy shopper? No one really knows.

CHAPTER 21

110

The Dollar General is in the York Square Shopping Center, at the corner of George Washington Memorial Highway and Denbigh Boulevard. The address is 2837 Denbigh Boulevard in Yorktown.

Regal Kiln Creek Stadium 20

Heading even farther to the outskirts of York County you will find a Regal Cinema theater on Victory Boulevard. I was speaking to one of the employees in August 2014, and she informed me that the theater had a phantom visitor who often makes himself known after hours. She told me that one night, while she was sweeping the aisles in one of the theaters, she heard a noise emitting from the projection room. She looked up and saw a dark silhouette passing by the projection window. All of the other employees were accounted for at the time, and none reported being in the projection room. A few other employees had similar encounters with this mysterious dark figure. She said that often the theater doors will close on their own when no one is around, and they will hear the sound of footsteps walking down the aisles in the theaters. I have been to this location several times, but have never experienced any paranormal activity. Perhaps I was never there late enough.

So there you have it ladies and gentlemen, some of the paranormal pit stops of Yorktown, Virginia. If you are in town and looking to spend the night, pick up some groceries, grab a bite to eat, or catch a movie, why do it alone when you can do it with a ghost?

Asfar, Dan. *Ghost Stories of Virginia*. Lone Pine Publishing, International, 1973.

Behrend, Jackie Eileen. *The Haunting of Williamsburg, Yorktown, and Jamestown*. John F. Blair Publishers, 1998.

Dupont Lee, Marguerite. *Virginia Ghosts*. Virginia Book Company, 1966.

Hatch, Charles E., Jr. *The Bellfield Estate*. National Park Service, 1970.

Hatch, Charles E., Jr. *York Under the Hill: Yorktown's Waterfront*. Colonial National Historical Park, 1973.

Hume, Ivor Noel. *Here Lies Virginia*. Alfred A. Knopf of New York, 1968.

Interview with employee (anonymous) of Carrot Tree Kitchens, 2012.

Interview with Linda Cassada, 2016.

Interview with Vivian Harris, 2016.

Ivy, Dick. *Fact Sheet of York County History*. York County Historical Committee, 2005.

National Park Service signs in Yorktown.

Taylor, L. B., Jr. *Ghosts of Virginia: Volume V*. Progress Printing Co., 2000.

Taylor, L. B., Jr. *Ghosts of Virginia: Volume VII*. Progress Printing Co., 2002.

Taylor, L. B., Jr. *The Ghosts of Williamsburg*. Progress Printing Co., 1992.

Trudell, Clyde. *Colonial Yorktown*. Thomas Publications, 1971.

Virginia Paranormal Investigations Case Files 2013–2016.

Websites:

www.DailyPress.com

www.msana.com

www.NPS.gov

www.VisitingYorktown.com

JEFF SANTOS came to Virginia and founded Virginia Paranormal Investigations in 2008. He has investigated several haunted locations throughout Virginia and the surrounding states, and his research has led him to find Yorktown steeped in paranormal activity, leading